VERSION CONTROL
by EXAMPLE

eric sink

pyrenean gold press

Version Control by Example
Copyright 2011 Eric Sink

Printed and bound in the United States of America 9 8 7 6 5 4 3 2

First edition: July 2011

Library of Congress Control Number: 2011935841

ISBN-13: 978-0-9835079-0-1

Editor: Brody Finney
Illustration, layout, and design: John Woolley

Pyrenean Gold Press
115 North Neil Street, Suite 408
Champaign, Illinois 61820
www.pyreneangoldpress.com

Ordering information: For details, contact the publisher at the address above.

Acknowledgments

I appreciate and want to acknowledge the efforts of those who helped me during the production of this book.

Two of my coworkers at SourceGear have been involved in this project in very substantial ways.

+ Everything about this book that *looks* good is a credit to John Woolley. And if there is anything about this book that does not look good, that was probably an area where I got in his way.

 John did the design, the layout, the illustrations, the cover, the font choices, everything.

 Personally, I think the book looks fantastic. My thanks to John Woolley.

+ The back of the title page lists Brody Finney as the "Editor" of this book, but that does not fully describe his contributions.

 While it is true that Brody's pedantry and red ink were critical, he and I also spent much time talking through issues of structure and content. He has been my sounding board on everything from British slang to the explanations of version control concepts.

 My thanks to Brody Finney for the many and varied ways that he made the content of this book better.

I received all kinds of helpful comments and constructive feedback from folks who read early drafts of this book.

+ My thanks to the following reviewers: Tom Alderman, Linda Bauer, Jonathan Blocksom, Rick Borup, Anthony Bova, Chris Bradley, Mark Brents, Brian Brewder, Andy Brice, Eli Carter, Fletcher Chambers, Michael Chermside, Steven Cherry, Zian Choy, Jeff Clausius, Jason Cohen, Ben Collins-Sussman, John Cook, Pascal Cuoq, Justin Davis,

Sybren Dijkstra, Augie Fackler, Emeric Fermas, Wez Furlong, Reggie Gardner, Rafał Grembowski, Fawad Halim, Michael Haren, Guy Harwood, Mark Heath, Kevin Horn, Jeff Hostetler, Kerry Jenkins, Joel Jirak, Zafiris Keramidas, Beth Kieler, Anthony Kirwan, Kristian Kristensen, Robert Lauer, Sasha Matijasic, Pierre Mengal, Gordon J Milne, Eamonn Murray, Dirkjan Ochtman, Ian Olsen, John O'Neill, Alex Papadimoulis, Dobrica Pavlinušić, Eric Peterson, Mike Pettypiece, C. Michael Pilato, Pavel Puchkarev, Sunil Puri, Joe Ream, Mike Reedell, Alvaro Rodriguez, Paul Roub, Michael Schoneman, Matt Schouten, J. Maximilian Spurk, Corey Steffen, Greg Stein, Scott Stocker, Jared Stofflett, Michael Third, Dixie Thornhill, Andy Tidball, Ben Tsai, Chuck Tuffli, Greg Vaughn, Wilbert van Dolleweerd, Stephen Ward, Rob Warner, Cullen Waters, Jason Webb, Robin Wilson

- My original plan was to keep this section of the acknowledgments very simple, like the alphabetical list above, with no attempt to describe how much feedback each person provided me.

  This plan was utterly ruined by Jakub Narębski, whose feedback during the editing process was extraordinary. He found errors no one else found. He gave me pages of background commentary. He wrote drafts of content he felt was too important not to cover.

  I appreciate the comments I received from **every** person who reviewed my book, but trust me on this one—Jakub's feedback was in a class by itself.

It takes a lot of focus to write a book. Several people supported me in the writing of this book by covering for my absence and offering me their patience. My thanks to:

- Ian Olsen, leader of the Veracity development team.
- Corey Steffen, my business partner.
- Lisa Sink, my wife; and Kellie and Lydia Sink, my daughters.

Finally, and above all, I express my gratitude to the Creator. I have been blessed. And I am thankful.

Contents

1   Introduction

A version control system is a piece of software that helps the developers on a software team work together and also archives a complete history of their work.

There are three basic goals of a version control system (VCS):

1. We want people to be able to work simultaneously, not serially.

    Think of your team as a multi-threaded piece of software with each developer running in his own thread. The key to high performance in a multi-threaded system is to maximize concurrency. Our goal is to never have a thread which is blocked on some other thread.

2. When people are working at the same time, we want their changes to not conflict with each other.

    Multi-threaded programming requires great care on the part of the developer and special features such as critical sections, locks, and a test-and-set instruction on the CPU. Without these kinds of things, the threads would overwrite each other's data. A multi-threaded software team needs things too, so that developers can work without messing each other up. That is what the version control system provides.

3. We want to archive every version of everything that has ever existed — ever.

    And who did it. And when. And why.

1. A History of Version Control

Broadly speaking, the history of version control tools can be divided into three generations.[1]

Table 1.1. Three Generations of Version Control

Generation	Networking	Operations	Concurrency	Examples
First	None	One file at a time	Locks	RCS, SCCS
Second	Centralized	Multi-file	Merge before commit	CVS, SourceSafe, Subversion, Team Foundation Server
Third	Distributed	Changesets	Commit before merge	Bazaar, Git, Mercurial

The forty year history of version control tools shows a steady movement toward more concurrency.

- In first generation tools, concurrent development was handled solely with locks. Only one person could be working on a file at a time.

- The second generation tools are a fair bit more permissive about simultaneous modifications, with one notable restriction. Users must merge the current revisions into their work before they are allowed to commit.

- The third generation tools allow merge and commit to be separated.

As I write this in mid-2011, the world of version control is in a time of transition. The vast majority of professional programmers are using second generation tools but the third generation is growing very quickly in popularity. The most popular VCS on Earth is Apache Subversion[2], an open source second generation tool. The high-end of the commercial market is dominated by IBM and Microsoft, both of which are firmly entrenched in second generation tools. But at the community level, where developers around the world talk about what's new and cool, the buzz is all about Distributed

---

[1] http://www.catb.org/~esr/writings/version-control/version-control.html — I don't remember for sure. I may have gotten this notion of three generations from Eric Raymond's "Understanding Version-Control Systems". Either way, it's a good read.

[2] http://subversion.apache.org/ — The proper name is "Apache Subversion", but in the interest of saving space, I'll be referring to it as simply "Subversion" throughout this book.

Version Control Systems (DVCS). The three most popular DVCS tools are Bazaar[3], Git[4] and Mercurial[5].

2. My Background

I am a software developer and entrepreneur. In 1997, I founded SourceGear, a software company which produces version control tools. I write occasionally on my blog at http://www.ericsink.com/. Version control tools have been an interest of mine for a very long time:

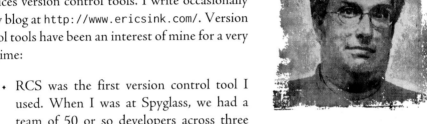

- RCS was the first version control tool I used. When I was at Spyglass, we had a team of 50 or so developers across three platforms using RCS on a shared code base. Since RCS never had support for networking, people on Windows and Mac had to log in to the Sun workstation that hosted RCS, FTP their code changes up there, and then check them in from the Unix shell. It was an interesting experience just trying to get all that to work. We Mac developers ended up writing a tool that sat on top of RCS to help us cope—we created a Mac application that shelled into a different server and did RCS stuff for us. We called that thing Norad. Don't ask me why we chose that name because I don't remember.

- At SourceGear, our first flagship product, SourceOffSite, was basically "Norad for SourceSafe". SourceSafe was kind of a generation 1.5 VCS. It was created by One Tree Software[6], a company that was acquired by Microsoft in 1994. SourceSafe had multiple-file operations, but no networking. We created SourceOffSite partially because our own team needed remote access to our SourceSafe repository. We released it as a product in 1998 and it became rather popular.

- And that brought us to our next endeavor, which was to build a version control system of our own. In 2003 we released Vault, a second generation tool designed specifically to be a replacement for SourceSafe. It provides SourceSafe users with a familiar experience and a seamless transition to a VCS with

---

[3]http://bazaar.canonical.com/en/
[4]http://git-scm.com/
[5]http://mercurial-scm.org/
[6]One Tree's founders included Brian Harry, who now leads the development of Microsoft Team Foundation Server.

full support for networking, atomic commits, and other second generation niceties. Vault has been our flagship product for most of the last decade and has been very successful.

+ In 2005, we created a division of SourceGear called Teamprise, focused on building Eclipse plugins for Microsoft Team Foundation Server. This business was acquired by Microsoft in 2009.

+ Our latest version control effort is a third generation tool called Veracity[7]. Veracity is open source.

3. Reading this book

First generation tools are mostly history at this point, so I won't be discussing them much.

I will cover the basics of version control with second generation tools in Part 1.

I will spend most of my pages talking about DVCS, the third generation tools. In Part 2, I will cover the same basics as before, but from a DVCS perspective. I also include some pros and cons for people who are making decisions about centralized vs. decentralized VCS solutions.

Note that the following four chapters are all very similar.

+ Chapter 3: *"Basics with Subversion"*
+ Chapter 7: *"Basics with Mercurial"*
+ Chapter 8: *"Basics with Git"*
+ Chapter 10: *"Basics with Veracity"*

These chapters walk through the same fictitious scenario using detailed examples, each with a different open source version control tool. Feel free to read the chapters corresponding to the tools that interest you most. Alternatively, you may want to read all four so that you can see how the various tools compare.

Finally, in Part 3, I will go a bit deeper. Learning about version control happens in two phases. In the first phase, the basics, we talk about "what".

+ What can we do with a VCS?
+ What commands are available?

---

[7]http://veracity-scm.com/

As we go deeper, we talk more about "how".

- How do we use a VCS?
- How should our development process work with a VCS?
- How does a VCS work?

Be advised that this book is written primarily for the command-line user. Topics like graphical user interfaces and integrated development environments are not covered here in this first edition. I did all the examples on a Mac, but all four of the version control tools covered in this book work well on Windows and Linux systems also.

The home page for this book is `http://www.ericsink.com/vcbe`

1

Centralized Version Control

2   Basics

There are 18 basic operations you can do with a version control system.[1] In this chapter, I will introduce each of these operations as an abstract notion which can be implemented by the actual commands of a specific version control tool. Usually, the name of my abstract operation is the most common name for the command that implements the operation. For example, since the action of committing changes to the repository is called "commit" by Subversion, Veracity, Git, Mercurial, and Bazaar, it seemed like a good idea to use that term here as well.

For the details of how these operations map to the concrete commands of specific version control tools, see later chapters, such as Chapter 3: *"Basics with Subversion"*.

1. Create
Create a new, empty repository.

A repository is the official place where you store all your work. It keeps track of your *tree*, by which I mean all your files, as well as the layout of the directories in which they are stored.

REPOSITORY

But there has to be more. If the definition in the previous paragraph were the whole story, then a version control repository would be no more than a network filesystem. A repository is much more than that. A repository contains history.

```
repository = filesystem * time
```

---

[1]Most version control systems have more than 18 commands, including lots of useful stuff I am not describing here. This chapter is about the 18 common operations which could be considered the core concepts of version control.

A filesystem is two-dimensional: Its space is defined by directories and files. In contrast, a repository is three-dimensional: It exists in a continuum defined by directories, files, and time. A version control repository contains every version of your source code that has ever existed.

A consequence of this idea is that nothing is ever really destroyed. Every time you make some kind of change to your repository, even if that change is to delete something, the repository gets larger because the history is longer. Each change adds to the history of the repository. We never subtract anything from that history.

The **create** operation is used to create a new repository. This is one of the first operations you will use, and after that, it gets used a lot less often.

When you create a new repository, your VCS will expect you to say something to identify it, such as where you want it to be created, or what its name should be.

2. Checkout
Create a working copy.

The **checkout** operation is used when you need to make a new working copy for a repository that already exists.

A working copy is a copy used for, er, working.

WORKING COPY

A working copy is a snapshot of the repository used by a developer as a place to make changes. The repository is shared by the whole team, but people do not modify it directly. Rather, each individual developer works by using a working copy. The working copy provides her with a private workspace where she can do her work isolated from the rest of the team.

The life of a developer is an infinite loop which looks something like this:

+ 10 Make a working copy of the contents of the repository.
+ 20 Modify the working copy.
+ 30 Modify the repository to incorporate those modifications.
+ 40 GOTO 20

Let's imagine for a moment what life would be like without this distinction between working copy and repository. In a single-person team, the situation could be described as tolerable. However, for any number of developers greater than one, things can get very messy.

I've seen people try it. They store their code on a file server. Everyone uses network file sharing and edits the source files in place. When somebody wants to edit main.cpp, they shout across the hall and ask if anybody else is using that file. Their Ethernet is saturated most of the time because the developers are actually compiling on their network drives.

With a version control tool, working on a multi-person team is much simpler. Each developer has a working copy to use as a private workspace. He can make changes to his own working copy without adversely affecting the rest of the team.

The working copy is actually more than just a snapshot of the contents of the repository. It also contains some metadata so that it can keep careful track of the state of things.

Let's suppose I have a brand new working copy. In other words, I started with nothing at all and I retrieved the latest versions from the repository. At this moment, my new working copy is completely synchronized with the contents of the repository. But that condition is not likely to last for long. I will be making changes to some of the files in this working copy so it will become newer than the repository. Other developers may be checking in their changes to the repository, thus making my working copy out of date. My working copy is going to be new and old at the same time. Things are going to get confusing. The version control tool is responsible for keeping track of everything. In fact, it must keep track of the state of each file individually.

For housekeeping purposes, the version control tool usually keeps a bit of extra information with the working copy. When a file is retrieved, the VCS stores its contents in the corresponding working copy of that file, but it also records certain information. For example:

- Your version control tool may record the timestamp on the working file so that it can later detect if you have modified it.

- It may record the version number of the repository file that was retrieved so that it may later know the starting point from which you began to make your changes.

- It may even tuck away a complete copy of the file that was retrieved so that it can show you a diff without accessing the server.

This stuff is stored in the *administrative area*, which is usually one or more hidden directories in the working copy. Its exact location depends on which version control tool you are using.

3. Commit

Apply the modifications in the working copy to the repository as a new changeset.

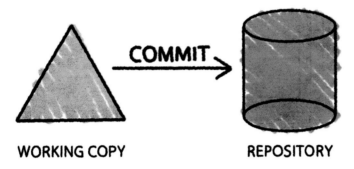

This is the operation that actually modifies the repository. Several others modify the working copy and add an operation to a list we call the *pending changeset*, a place where changes wait to be committed. The **commit** operation takes the pending changeset and uses it to create a new version of the tree in the repository.

All modern version control tools perform this operation atomically. In other words, no matter how many individual modifications are in your pending changeset, the repository will either end up with all of them (if the operation is successful), or none of them (if the operation fails). It is impossible for the repository to end up in a state with only half of the operations done. The integrity of the repository is assured.

It is typical to provide a log message (or comment) when you commit, explaining the changes you have made. This log message becomes part of the history of the repository.

4. Update

Update the working copy with respect to the repository.

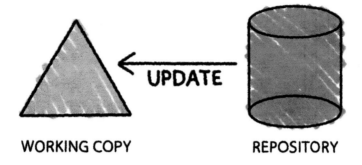

WORKING COPY   **REPOSITORY**

Update brings your working copy up-to-date by applying changes from the repository, merging them with any changes you have made to your working copy if necessary. When the working copy was first created, its contents exactly reflected a specific revision of the repository. The VCS remembers that revision so that it can keep careful track of where you started making your changes. This revision is often referred to as the *parent* of the working copy, because if you commit changes from the working copy, that revision will be the parent of the new changeset.[2]

Update is sort of like the mirror image of **commit**. Both operations move changes between the working copy and the repository. **Commit** goes from the working copy to the repository. **Update** goes in the other direction.

---

[2]Speaking generally, the **update** operation is used to change the parent of the working copy, most commonly moving it forward so that the working copy contains the most recent changes in the repository.

5. Add
Add a file or directory.

Use the **add** operation when you have a file or directory in your working copy that is not yet under version control and you want to add it to the repository. The item is not actually added immediately. Rather, the item becomes part of the pending changeset, and is added to the repository when you commit.

6. Edit
Modify a file.

This is the most common operation when using a version control system. When you checkout, your working copy contains a bunch of files from the repository. You modify those files, expecting to make your changes a part of the repository.

With most version control tools, the **edit** operation doesn't actually involve the VCS directly. You simply edit the file using your favorite text editor or development environment and the VCS will notice the change and make the modified file part of the pending changeset.

On the other hand, some version control tools want you to be more explicit. Such tools usually set the filesystem read-only bit on all files in the working copy. Later, when you notify the VCS that you want to modify a file, it will make the working copy of that file writable.

7. Delete
Delete a file or directory.

Use the **delete** operation when you want to remove a file or directory from the repository.

If you try to delete a file which has been modified in your working copy, your VCS might complain.

Typically, the **delete** operation will immediately delete the working copy of the file, but the actual deletion of the file in the repository is simply added to the pending changeset.

Recall that in the repository the file is not really deleted. When you commit a changeset containing a delete, you are simply creating a new version of the tree which does not contain the deleted file. The previous version of the tree is still in the repository, and that version still contains the file.

8. Rename
Rename a file or directory.

Use the **rename** operation when you want to change the name of a file or directory. The operation is added to the pending changeset, but the item in the working copy typically gets renamed immediately.

There is lot of variety in how version control tools support rename. Some of the earlier tools had no support for rename at all.

Some tools (including Bazaar and Veracity) implement rename formally, requiring that they be notified explicitly when something is to be renamed. Such tools treat the name of a file or directory as simply one of its attributes, subject to change over time.

Still other tools (including Git) implement rename informally, detecting renames by observing changes rather than by keeping track of the identity of a file. Rename detection usually works well in practice, but if a file has been both renamed and modified, there is a chance the VCS will do the wrong thing.

9. Move
Move a file or directory.

Use the **move** operation when you want to move a file or directory from one place in the tree to another. The operation is added to the pending changeset, but the item in the working copy typically gets moved immediately.

Some tools treat **rename** and **move** as the same operation (in the Unix tradition of treating the file's entire path as its name), while others keep them separate (by thinking of the file's name and its containing directory as separate attributes).

10. Status
List the modifications that have been made to the working copy.

As you make changes in your working copy, each change is added to the pending changeset. The **status** operation is used to see the pending changeset. Or to put it another way, **status** shows you what changes would be applied to the repository if you were to commit.

11. Diff

Show the details of the modifications that have been made to the working copy.

Status provides a list of changes but no details about them. To see exactly what changes have been made to the files, you need to use the **diff** operation. Your VCS may implement diff in a number of different ways. For a command-line application, it may simply print out a diff to the console. Or your VCS might launch a visual diff application.

12. Revert

Undo modifications that have been made to the working copy.

Sometimes I make changes to my working copy that I simply don't intend to keep. Perhaps I tried to fix a bug and discovered that my fix introduced five new bugs which are worse than the one I started with. Or perhaps I just changed my mind. In any case, a very nice feature of a working copy is the ability to revert the changes I have made.

A complete revert of the working copy will throw away all your pending changes and return the working copy to the way it was just after you did the checkout.

13. Log

Show the history of changes to the repository.

Your repository keeps track of every version that has ever existed. The **log** operation is the way to see those records. It displays each changeset along with additional data such as:

+ Who made the change?

+ When was the change made?

+ What was the log message?

1503 - began
1519 - completed
1809 - cleaned
1911 - stolen
1913 - recovered
1956 - damaged
2011 - fedora

Most version control tools present ways of slicing and dicing this information. For example, you can ask **log** to list all the changesets made by the user named Leonardo, or all the changesets made during April 2010.

14. Tag

Associate a meaningful name with a specific version in the repository.

Version control tools provide a way to mark a specific instant in the history of the repository with a meaningful name.

This is not altogether different from the descriptive and memorable names we use for variables and constants in our code. Which of the following two lines of code is easier to understand?

```
if (-43 == e)
if (ERR_FILE_NOT_FOUND == errorcode)
```

Similarly, which of the following is the most intuitive?

```
378
eb1637d58b1bd8f253a2f3610e8e5a7050a434ec
LAST_VERSION_BEFORE_COREY_FOULED_EVERYTHING_UP
```

15. Branch
Create another line of development.

The **branch** operation is what you use when you want your development process to fork off into two different directions. For example, when you release version 3.0, you might want to create a branch so that development of 4.0 features can be kept separate from 3.0.x bug-fixes.

16. Merge
Apply changes from one branch to another.

Typically when you have used **branch** to enable your development to diverge, you later want it to converge again, at least partially. For example, if you created a branch for 3.0.x bug-fixes, you probably want those bug-fixes to happen in the main line of development as well. Without the **merge** operation, you could still achieve this by manually doing the bug-fixes in both branches. **Merge** makes this operation simpler by automating things as much as possible.

17. Resolve
Handle conflicts resulting from a merge.

In some cases, the **merge** operation requires human intervention. **Merge** automatically deals with everything that can be done safely. Everything else is considered a *conflict*. For example, what if the file foo.js was modified in one branch and deleted in the other? This kind of situation requires a person to make the decisions. The **resolve** operation is used to help the user figure things out and to inform the VCS how the conflict should be handled.

18. Lock
Prevent other people from modifying a file.

The **lock** operation is used to get exclusive rights to modify a file. Not all version control tools include this feature. In some cases, it is provided but is intended to be rarely used. For any files that are in a format based on plain text (source code, XML, etc.), it is usually best to just let the VCS handle the concurrency issues. But for binary files which cannot be automatically merged, it can be handy to grab a lock on a file.

3   Basics with Subversion

Futilisoft has begun work on a new product. This product calculates the probability (as an integer percentage) of winning the Powerball for any given set of numbers.

> Powerball[1] is a lottery in the United States. It involves drawing five white balls and one red ball, sometimes called the "power ball".

The company has assigned two developers to work on this new project, Harry, located in Birmingham, England, and Sally, located in Birmingham, Alabama. Both developers are telecommuting to the Futilisoft corporate headquarters in Cleveland. After a bit of discussion, they have decided to implement their product as a command-line app in C and to use Apache Subversion[2] 1.6.15 for version control.

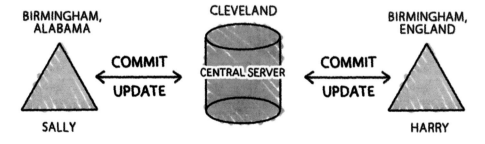

---

[1] http://powerball.com/
[2] http://subversion.apache.org/

1. Create

Sally gets the project started by creating a new repository.

```
~ server$ cd

~ server$ mkdir repos

~ server$ svnadmin create repos/lottery

~ server$ svnserve -d --root=/Users/sally/repos
```

I consider the details of server configuration to be too esoteric for this book. So you can just assume that it happened here. Magically…

2. Checkout, Add, Status, Commit

By this time Harry is back from his tea and is ready to create a working copy and start coding.

```
~ harry$ svn checkout svn://server.futilisoft.com/lottery
Checked out revision 0.
```

Harry wonders if Sally has already done anything in the new repository.

```
~ harry$ cd lottery

lottery harry$ ls -al
total 0
drwxr-xr-x  3 harry  staff  102 Apr  6 11:40 .
drwxr-xr-x  3 harry  staff  102 Apr  6 11:40 ..
drwxr-xr-x  7 harry  staff  238 Apr  6 11:40 .svn
```

Apparently not. Nothing here but the .svn administrative area. Jolly good then. It's time to start coding. He opens his text editor and creates the starting point for their product.

```
#include <stdio.h>
#include <stdlib.h>

int calculate_result(int white_balls[5], int power_ball)
```

```
{
    return 0;
}

int main(int argc, char** argv)
{
    if (argc != 7)
    {
        fprintf(stderr, "Usage: %s power_ball (5 white balls)\n", argv[0]);
        return -1;
    }

    int power_ball = atoi(argv[1]);

    int white_balls[5];
    for (int i=0; i<5; i++)
    {
        white_balls[i] = atoi(argv[2+i]);
    }

    int result = calculate_result(white_balls, power_ball);

    printf("%d percent chance of winning\n", result);

    return 0;
}
```

Typical of most initial implementations, this is missing a lot of features. But it's a good place to begin. Before committing his code, he wants to make sure it compiles and runs.

```
lottery harry$ gcc -std=c99 lottery.c

lottery harry$ ls -l
total 32
-rwxr-xr-x  1 harry  staff  8904 Apr  6 12:15 a.out
-rw-r--r--  1 harry  staff   555 Apr  6 12:15 lottery.c

lottery harry$ ./a.out
Usage: ./a.out power_ball (5 white balls)

lottery harry$ ./a.out 42 1 2 3 4 5
0 percent chance of winning
```

Righto. Time to store this file in the repository. First Harry needs to add the file to the pending changeset.

```
lottery harry$ svn add lottery.c
A         lottery.c
```

Harry uses the status operation to make sure the pending changeset looks proper.

```
lottery harry$ svn status
?       a.out
A       lottery.c
```

Subversion is complaining because it doesn't know what to do about that a.out file. That's a compiled executable, which should not be stored in a version control repository. Keep calm and carry on. Now it's time to commit the file.

```
lottery harry$ svn commit -m "initial implementation"
Adding          lottery.c
Transmitting file data .
Committed revision 1.
```

> *Using the -m flag with **svn commit** is actually not a typical way of specifying the commit log message. Many folks just **svn commit** and then Subversion will bring up a text editor where they can type a multi-line comment. But that action is awkward to illustrate here in a book, so I'm just pretending that -m is typical usage.*

3. Log, Diff

Now Sally needs to set up her own working copy.

```
~ sally$ svn checkout svn://server.futilisoft.com/lottery
A    lottery/lottery.c
Checked out revision 1.

~ sally$ ls -l lottery
total 8
-rw-r--r-- 1 sally  staff  555 Apr  6 12:41 lottery.c
```

When she sees that Harry has checked in the initial code they had previously discussed, Sally is happy as a coyote in the hen house. She wants to check the log to see the details.

```
~ sally$ cd lottery

lottery sally$ svn log
------------------------------------------------------------------------
r1 | harry | 2011-04-06 12:32:46 -0500 (Wed, 06 Apr 2011) | 1 line

initial implementation
------------------------------------------------------------------------
```

When Sally decides to take a look at the code, she immediately finds something that makes her nervous as a long-tailed cat in a room full of rockin' chairs. The program expects the red ball number to be the first argument, followed by the other five. But in the actual lottery, the five white numbers are always drawn and shown first. She worries this will be confusing for users so she decides to fix it. Fortunately it is only necessary to modify a few lines of main().

```c
    if (argc != 7)
    {
        fprintf(stderr, "Usage: %s (5 white balls) power_ball\n", argv[0]);
        return -1;
    }

    int power_ball = atoi(argv[6]);

    int white_balls[5];
    for (int i=0; i<5; i++)
    {
        white_balls[i] = atoi(argv[1+i]);
    }
```

Now she wants to use the **status** operation to see the pending changes.

```
lottery sally$ svn status
M       lottery.c
```

No surprise there. Subversion knows that lottery.c has been modified. She wants to double-check by reviewing the actual changes.

```
lottery sally$ svn diff
Index: lottery.c
===================================================================
--- lottery.c   (revision 1)
+++ lottery.c   (working copy)
@@ -11,16 +11,16 @@
 {
     if (argc != 7)
     {
-        fprintf(stderr, "Usage: %s power_ball (5 white balls)\n", argv[0]);
```

```
+        fprintf(stderr, "Usage: %s (5 white balls) power_ball\n", argv[0]);
         return -1;
    }

-   int power_ball = atoi(argv[1]);
+   int power_ball = atoi(argv[6]);

    int white_balls[5];
    for (int i=0; i<5; i++)
    {
-       white_balls[i] = atoi(argv[2+i]);
+       white_balls[i] = atoi(argv[1+i]);
    }

    int result = calculate_result(white_balls, power_ball);
```

Ain't that the berries!?!

> *The basic **svn diff** command dumps output to the console in a format which is familiar to users of the standard Unix diff command. That's the convention I'm using in this chapter. However, many users configure Subversion to bring up a visual diff app instead.*

4. Update, Commit (with a merge)

Meanwhile, Harry has been coding as well. He heard somebody say that it's best to compile with all the warnings turned on, so he decides to give it a try.

```
lottery harry$ gcc -std=c99 -Wall -Wextra -Werror lottery.c
cc1: warnings being treated as errors
lottery.c:5: warning: unused parameter 'white_balls'
lottery.c:5: warning: unused parameter 'power_ball'
```

I say! The code has some warnings. The calculate_result() function isn't using its parameters. Harry looks at the situation and realises the problem immediately: That function should be checking its arguments for validity! The power ball can be from 1 to 39 inclusive. The white balls can be 1 to 59 inclusive. So he implements the error checking.

```
int calculate_result(int white_balls[5], int power_ball)
{
    for (int i=0; i<5; i++)
    {
        if (
            (white_balls[i] < 1)
            || (white_balls[i] > 59)
          )
        {
            return -1;
        }
    }

    if (
        (power_ball < 1)
        || (power_ball > 39)
      )
    {
        return -1;
    }

    return 0;
}
```

Grand. Let's see if it compiles.

```
lottery harry$ gcc -std=c99 -Wall -Wextra -Werror lottery.c

lottery harry$ ls -l
total 32
-rwxr-xr-x  1 harry  staff  8904 Apr  6 13:23 a.out
-rw-r--r--  1 harry  staff   843 Apr  6 13:21 lottery.c
```

Quite. But Harry decides to diff before committing, just for good measure.

```
lottery harry$ svn diff
Index: lottery.c
===================================================================
--- lottery.c   (revision 1)
+++ lottery.c   (working copy)
@@ -4,6 +4,25 @@

 int calculate_result(int white_balls[5], int power_ball)
 {
+    for (int i=0; i<5; i++)
+    {
+        if (
+            (white_balls[i] < 1)
+            || (white_balls[i] > 59)
+          )
+        {
+            return -1;
```

```
+          }
+      }
+
+      if (
+          (power_ball < 1)
+          || (power_ball > 39)
+      )
+      {
+          return -1;
+      }
+
       return 0;
 }
```

Good show. Time to commit the change.

But Sally has been working at the same time and she had her change ready to commit first.

```
lottery sally$ svn commit -m "change order of the command line args to be \
                                more like what the user will expect"
Sending         lottery.c
Transmitting file data .
Committed revision 2.
```

Just after Sally commits her changes, Harry tries to commit his.

```
lottery harry$ svn commit -m "fix some warnings"
Sending         lottery.c
Transmitting file data .svn: Commit failed (details follow):
svn: File '/lottery.c' is out of date
```

What's all this then? Subversion is not allowing Harry to commit his change because it was based on a no-longer-current revision of lottery.c.

This behavior on the part of Subversion is typical for a second generation VCS. The model is sometimes called "edit-merge-commit", because it often requires the user to do a merge before they are allowed to commit.

Harry uses update to make his working copy current.

```
lottery harry$ svn update
G    lottery.c
Updated to revision 2.
```

> *In this case, the update went fine, and Harry is able to go forward without much trouble. But if things go badly, his working copy becomes a mixture of his changes all stirred up with the changes being merged in from the repository. If he has trouble with the merge, it will be difficult for him to back out and try again without losing his own work. This issue is a major problem with the way second generation tools handle merging.*

Everything seems to be ship-shape and Bristol fashion. The 'G' next to lottery.c means that the file has been merged. Harry wants to see what happened.

```
lottery harry$ svn diff
Index: lottery.c
===================================================================
--- lottery.c   (revision 2)
+++ lottery.c   (working copy)
@@ -4,6 +4,25 @@

 int calculate_result(int white_balls[5], int power_ball)
 {
+    for (int i=0; i<5; i++)
+    {
+        if (
+            (white_balls[i] < 1)
+            || (white_balls[i] > 59)
+        )
+        {
+            return -1;
+        }
+    }
+
+    if (
+        (power_ball < 1)
+        || (power_ball > 39)
+    )
+    {
+        return -1;
```

```
+    }
+
     return 0;
 }
```

Interesting. Diff still shows only Harry's changes. But the baseline version of lottery.c now shows "(revision 2)", whereas in the previous diff it showed "(revision 1)". Harry decides to peek inside the file and discovers that main() has some new code in it. That must have come from Sally (who else?), and apparently Subversion was able to merge Sally's changes directly into Harry's modified copy of the file without any conflicts. Smashing! Still, what was the purpose of these changes?

```
lottery harry$ svn log
------------------------------------------------------------------------
r2 | sally | 2011-04-06 13:26:47 -0500 (Wed, 06 Apr 2011) | 1 line

change order of the command line args to be more like what the user will expect
------------------------------------------------------------------------
r1 | harry | 2011-04-06 12:32:46 -0500 (Wed, 06 Apr 2011) | 1 line

initial implementation
------------------------------------------------------------------------
```

Ah. Very well then. So Harry tries the commit once again.

```
lottery harry$ svn commit -m "fix some warnings"
Sending        lottery.c
Transmitting file data .
Committed revision 3.
```

5. Update (with merge)

Meanwhile, Sally is fixin' to go ahead and add a feature that was requested by the sales team: If the user chooses the lucky number 7 as the red ball, the chances of winning are doubled. Since she is starting a new task, she decides to begin with an update to make sure she has the latest code.

```
lottery sally$ svn update
U    lottery.c
Updated to revision 3.
```

Then she implements the lucky 7 feature in two shakes of a lamb's tail by adding just a few lines of new code to main().

```
lottery sally$ svn diff
Index: lottery.c
===================================================================
--- lottery.c    (revision 3)
+++ lottery.c    (working copy)
@@ -44,6 +44,11 @@

      int result = calculate_result(white_balls, power_ball);

+     if (7 == power_ball)
+     {
+         result = result * 2;
+     }
+
      printf("%d percent chance of winning\n", result);

      return 0;
```

And commits her change.

```
lottery sally$ svn commit -m "lucky 7"
Sending        lottery.c
Transmitting file data .
Committed revision 4.
```

Meanwhile, Harry has realised his last change had a bug. He modified calcu-late_result() to return -1 for invalid arguments but he forgot to modify the caller to handle the error. As a consequence, entering a ball number that is out of range causes the program to behave improperly.

```
lottery harry$ ./a.out 61 2 3 4 5 42
-1 percent chance of winning
```

The percent chance of winning certainly can't be a negative number, now can it? So Harry adds an extra check for this case.

```
lottery harry$ svn diff
Index: lottery.c
===================================================================
--- lottery.c    (revision 3)
+++ lottery.c    (working copy)
@@ -44,6 +44,12 @@

      int result = calculate_result(white_balls, power_ball);

+     if (result < 0)
+     {
+         fprintf(stderr, "Invalid arguments\n");
+         return -1;
```

```
+    }
+
     printf("%d percent chance of winning\n", result);

     return 0;
```

And proceeds to commit the fix.

```
lottery harry$ svn commit -m "propagate error code"
Sending        lottery.c
Transmitting file data .svn: Commit failed (details follow):
svn: File '/lottery.c' is out of date
```

Blimey! Sally must have committed a new changeset already. Harry once again needs to do an update to merge Sally's changes with his own.

```
lottery harry$ svn update
Conflict discovered in 'lottery.c'.
Select: (p) postpone, (df) diff-full, (e) edit,
        (mc) mine-conflict, (tc) theirs-conflict,
        (s) show all options:
```

The merge didn't go quite as smoothly this time. Apparently there was a conflict. Harry wonders if he could sneak out for a pint. Instead, Harry chooses the (df) option to review the conflicting changes.

```
lottery harry$ svn update
Conflict discovered in 'lottery.c'.
Select: (p) postpone, (df) diff-full, (e) edit,
        (mc) mine-conflict, (tc) theirs-conflict,
        (s) show all options: df
--- .svn/text-base/lottery.c.svn-base   Wed Apr  6 14:07:48 2011
+++ .svn/tmp/lottery.c.2.tmp    Wed Apr  6 19:53:26 2011
@@ -44,6 +44,20 @@

     int result = calculate_result(white_balls, power_ball);

+<<<<<<< .mine
+    if (result < 0)
+    {
+        fprintf(stderr, "Invalid arguments\n");
+        return -1;
+    }
+
+=======
+    if (7 == power_ball)
+    {
+        result = result * 2;
+    }
+
```

```
+>>>>>>> .r4
    printf("%d percent chance of winning\n", result);

    return 0;
Select: (p) postpone, (df) diff-full, (e) edit, (r) resolved,
        (mc) mine-conflict, (tc) theirs-conflict,
        (s) show all options:
```

Just like that. A conflict. Harry decides to (p) postpone it so he can look at the problem more carefully.

```
Select: (p) postpone, (df) diff-full, (e) edit, (r) resolved,
        (mc) mine-conflict, (tc) theirs-conflict,
        (s) show all options: p
C    lottery.c
Updated to revision 4.
Summary of conflicts:
  Text conflicts: 1
```

Now he opens lottery.c in his editor to examine the situation.

```
...
    int result = calculate_result(white_balls, power_ball);

<<<<<<< .mine
    if (result < 0)
    {
        fprintf(stderr, "Invalid arguments\n");
        return -1;
    }

=======

    if (7 == power_ball)
    {
        result = result * 2;
    }

>>>>>>> .r4
    printf("%d percent chance of winning\n", result);

    return 0;
...
```

Subversion has included both Harry's code and Sally's code with conflict markers to delimit things. It appears that Sally's new code can simply be included right after Harry's error checking. So in this case, resolving the conflict is frightfully simple. Harry just removes the lines containing the conflict markers.

```
...
    int result = calculate_result(white_balls, power_ball);

    if (result < 0)
    {
        fprintf(stderr, "Invalid arguments\n");
        return -1;
    }

    if (7 == power_ball)
    {
        result = result * 2;
    }

    printf("%d percent chance of winning\n", result);

    return 0;
...
```

That should take care of the problem. Harry compiles the code to make sure and then retries the commit.

```
lottery harry$ svn commit -m "propagate error code"
svn: Commit failed (details follow):
svn: Aborting commit: '/Users/harry/lottery/lottery.c' remains in conflict
```

Crikey! Howzat? Harry fixed the conflict in lottery.c but Subversion doesn't seem to know that.

```
lottery harry$ svn status
?       a.out
?       lottery.c.r3
?       lottery.c.r4
?       lottery.c.mine
C       lottery.c
```

Harry sees that 'C' next to lottery.c and realises that he forgot to tell Subversion that he had resolved the conflict. He uses **resolve** to let Subversion know that the problem has been dealt with.

```
lottery harry$ svn resolve --accept=working lottery.c
Resolved conflicted state of 'lottery.c'

lottery harry$ svn status
?       a.out
M       lottery.c
```

There, that looks much better. Harry tries the commit for the third time.

```
lottery harry$ svn commit -m "propagate error code"
Sending        lottery.c
Transmitting file data .
Committed revision 5.
```

And... Bob's your uncle.

6. Move

Harry immediately moves on to his next task, which is to put the repository into the recommended structure[3].

```
lottery harry$ mkdir trunk

lottery harry$ svn add trunk
A         trunk

lottery harry$ svn move lottery.c trunk
A         trunk/lottery.c
D         lottery.c

lottery harry$ mkdir branches

lottery harry$ svn add branches
A         branches

lottery harry$ svn st
D         lottery.c
A         trunk
A   +     trunk/lottery.c
A         branches

lottery harry$ svn commit -m "recommended dir structure"
Adding          branches
Deleting        lottery.c
Adding          trunk
Adding          trunk/lottery.c

Committed revision 6.
```

---

[3]For Subversion and other tools which represent branches as directories, it is considered good practice to keep the trunk at the top level of the tree alongside a directory into which branches are placed.

> *Ouch. Subversion's move command (which is also used for rename) appears to be implemented as an add and a delete. This makes me worry that the upcoming merge is not going to go smoothly.*

Sally decides having the number 7 as a constant in the code is as ugly as homemade soap. She adds a #define to give it a more meaningful name.

```
lottery sally$ svn diff
Index: lottery.c
=================================================================
--- lottery.c   (revision 5)
+++ lottery.c   (working copy)
@@ -2,6 +2,8 @@
 #include <stdio.h>
 #include <stdlib.h>

+#define LUCKY_NUMBER 7
+
 int calculate_result(int white_balls[5], int power_ball)
 {
     for (int i=0; i<5; i++)
@@ -50,7 +52,7 @@
         return -1;
     }

-    if (7 == power_ball)
+    if (LUCKY_NUMBER == power_ball)
     {
         result = result * 2;
     }
```

And immediately tries to commit the change.

```
lottery sally$ svn commit -m "use a #define for the lucky number"
Sending        lottery.c
Transmitting file data .svn: (Commit failed) (details follow):
svn: File not found: transaction '6-8', path '/lottery.c'
```

But Subversion says "File not found"? What in the Sam Hill is that? Sally tries an update.

```
lottery sally$ svn update
   C lottery.c
A    trunk
A    trunk/lottery.c
```

```
A    branches
Updated to revision 6.
Summary of conflicts:
  Tree conflicts: 1

lottery sally$ svn st
A  +  C lottery.c
      >    local edit, incoming delete upon update
```

Tree conflict? "Incoming delete upon update"? Sally wonders if she could sneak out for some collard greens.

> *Subversion failed to merge the changes from Sally's working copy into the moved file. I was sort of expecting this when I saw earlier that Subversion was showing the move as an add/delete.*

Apparently lottery.c has moved into a subdirectory called trunk. Sally remembers discussing this with Harry. So she re-applies her #define changes to the new lottery.c in trunk.

```
lottery sally$ svn st
A  +  C lottery.c
      >    local edit, incoming delete upon update
M       trunk/lottery.c
```

Now **svn status** shows the edits she just made, but it's still bellyaching about conflicts with the old lottery.c. That file isn't supposed to exist anymore. Since her changes have now been made in the new lottery.c, she decides to revert her changes to the old one.

```
lottery sally$ svn revert lottery.c
Reverted 'lottery.c'

lottery sally$ svn st
?       lottery.c
M       trunk/lottery.c

lottery sally$ rm lottery.c
```

That resulted in svn status saying ?, so she just deletes her working copy of the file.

Now diff shows her changes applied to the new copy.

```
lottery sally$ svn diff
Index: trunk/lottery.c
===================================================================
--- trunk/lottery.c (revision 6)
+++ trunk/lottery.c (working copy)
@@ -2,6 +2,8 @@
 #include <stdio.h>
 #include <stdlib.h>

+#define LUCKY_NUMBER 7
+
 int calculate_result(int white_balls[5], int power_ball)
 {
     for (int i=0; i<5; i++)
@@ -50,7 +52,7 @@
         return -1;
     }

-    if (7 == power_ball)
+    if (LUCKY_NUMBER == power_ball)
     {
         result = result * 2;
     }
```

And she is ready to commit.

```
lottery sally$ svn commit -m "use a #define for the lucky number"
Sending        trunk/lottery.c
Transmitting file data .
Committed revision 7.
```

7. Rename

Harry decides the time has come to create a proper `Makefile`. And also to gratuitously rename `lottery.c`.

```
trunk harry$ svn add Makefile
A         Makefile

trunk harry$ svn move lottery.c pb.c
A         pb.c
D         lottery.c

trunk harry$ svn commit -m "Makefile. and lottery.c was too long to type."
Adding         trunk/Makefile
```

```
Deleting        trunk/lottery.c
Adding          trunk/pb.c
Transmitting file data .
Committed revision 8.
```

Sally maintains her momentum with #define and adds names for the ball ranges.

```
trunk sally$ svn diff
Index: lottery.c
===============================================================
--- lottery.c   (revision 7)
+++ lottery.c   (working copy)
@@ -3,6 +3,8 @@
 #include <stdlib.h>

 #define LUCKY_NUMBER 7
+#define MAX_WHITE_BALL 59
+#define MAX_POWER_BALL 39

 int calculate_result(int white_balls[5], int power_ball)
 {
@@ -10,7 +12,7 @@
     {
         if (
             (white_balls[i] < 1)
-            || (white_balls[i] > 59)
+            || (white_balls[i] > MAX_WHITE_BALL)
         )
         {
             return -1;
@@ -19,7 +21,7 @@

     if (
         (power_ball < 1)
-        || (power_ball > 39)
+        || (power_ball > MAX_POWER_BALL)
     )
     {
         return -1;
```

And commits her changes.

```
trunk sally$ svn commit -m "more #defines"
Sending        trunk/lottery.c
Transmitting file data .svn: Commit failed (details follow):
svn: File not found: transaction '8-b', path '/trunk/lottery.c'
```

Grrr. Tree conflict problem again. That Harry is dumber than a box of rocks. This looks a lot like the last problem she had, so she figures it'll get fixed the same way.

```
trunk sally$ svn update
   C lottery.c
A    pb.c
A    Makefile
Updated to revision 8.
Summary of conflicts:
  Tree conflicts: 1

trunk sally$ svn st
M       pb.c
A  +  C lottery.c
      >    local edit, incoming delete upon update

trunk sally$ svn revert lottery.c
Reverted 'lottery.c'

trunk sally$ svn st
?       lottery.c
M       pb.c

trunk sally$ rm lottery.c

trunk sally$ svn st
M       pb.c
```

Even though Subversion did not handle this incoming rename merge gracefully, it is interesting to note that it correctly produced pb.c, complete with Sally's changes in it.

```
trunk sally$ svn commit -m "more #defines"
Sending        trunk/pb.c
Transmitting file data .
Committed revision 9.
```

8. Delete

Harry wants to get a head start on Zawinski's Law, so he decides to add an IMAP protocol library to their tree.

> *As spoken by the legendary Jamie Zawinski*[4]:
> *"Every program attempts to expand until it can read mail. Those programs which cannot so expand are replaced by ones which can."*

```
trunk harry$ svn commit -m "add libvmime so we can do the mail reader feature"
Adding          trunk/libvmime-0.9.1
Adding          trunk/libvmime-0.9.1/AUTHORS
Adding          trunk/libvmime-0.9.1/COPYING
Adding          trunk/libvmime-0.9.1/ChangeLog
Adding          trunk/libvmime-0.9.1/HACKING
Adding          trunk/libvmime-0.9.1/INSTALL
Adding          trunk/libvmime-0.9.1/Makefile.am
...
Transmitting file data ..........................................
Committed revision 10.
```

Sally does an update and finds something that reminds her of what comes out of the south end of a northbound dog.

```
trunk sally$ svn update
A    libvmime-0.9.1
A    libvmime-0.9.1/vmime.vcproj
A    libvmime-0.9.1/README.refcounting
A    libvmime-0.9.1/m4
A    libvmime-0.9.1/m4/lib-link.m4
A    libvmime-0.9.1/m4/lib-prefix.m4
A    libvmime-0.9.1/m4/acx_pthread.m4
A    libvmime-0.9.1/m4/lib-ld.m4
A    libvmime-0.9.1/m4/libgnutls.m4
...
Updated to revision 10.
```

Sally remembers that the specification says the product isn't supposed to include a full email reader until the next release. For the entire 1.0 development cycle, that third party library is going to be about as useful as a trap door in a canoe. So she deletes it.

```
trunk sally$ svn delete libvmime-0.9.1
D    libvmime-0.9.1/vmime.vcproj
D    libvmime-0.9.1/README.refcounting
D    libvmime-0.9.1/m4/lib-link.m4
```

---

[4]http://www.jwz.org/blog/

```
D         libvmime-0.9.1/m4/lib-prefix.m4
D         libvmime-0.9.1/m4/acx_pthread.m4
D         libvmime-0.9.1/m4/lib-ld.m4
D         libvmime-0.9.1/m4/libgnutls.m4
...

trunk sally$ svn commit -m "no mail reader until 2.0"
Deleting        trunk/libvmime-0.9.1

Committed revision 11.
```

9. Lock, Revert

Fed up with conflicts, Sally decides to lock pb.c so only she can modify it.

```
trunk sally$ svn lock pb.c
'pb.c' locked by user 'sally'.
```

Harry does an update.

```
trunk harry$ svn update
U    pb.c
D    libvmime-0.9.1
Updated to revision 11.

trunk harry$ ls
Makefile    pb.c

trunk harry$ ls -l
total 16
-rw-r--r--  1 harry  staff    58 Apr  7 08:13 Makefile
-rw-r--r--  1 harry  staff  1121 Apr  7 08:51 pb.c
```

Blast! That daft Sally deleted all his email code! Harry decides to indent[5] pb.c.

```
trunk harry$ indent pb.c

trunk harry$ svn st
?         pb.c.BAK
M         pb.c

trunk harry$ svn commit -m "indent pb.c"
Sending         trunk/pb.c
Transmitting file data .svn: Commit failed (details follow):
svn: User harry does not own lock on path '/trunk/pb.c' (currently locked by sally)
```

---

[5]http://en.wikipedia.org/wiki/Indent_(Unix)

What a kerfuffle. Harry reverts the changes.

```
trunk harry$ svn revert pb.c
Reverted 'pb.c'

trunk harry$ svn st
?       pb.c.BAK

trunk harry$ rm pb.c.BAK
```

Sally, basking in the comfort of her lock, makes her edits. She has decided to eliminate uses of `atoi()`, which is deprecated.

```
trunk sally$ svn diff
Index: pb.c
===================================================================
--- pb.c    (revision 10)
+++ pb.c    (working copy)
@@ -43,7 +43,14 @@
        int white_balls[5];
        for (int i=0; i<5; i++)
        {
-           white_balls[i] = atoi(argv[1+i]);
+           char* endptr = NULL;
+           long val = strtol(argv[1+i], &endptr, 10);
+           if (*endptr)
+           {
+               fprintf(stderr, "Invalid arguments\n");
+               return -1;
+           }
+           white_balls[i] = (int) val;
        }

        int result = calculate_result(white_balls, power_ball);

trunk sally$ make
gcc -std=c99 -Wall -Wextra -Werror pb.c -o pb

trunk sally$ ./pb 1 2 3 4 5 6
0 percent chance of winning

trunk sally$ ./pb 1 2 3e 4 5 6
Invalid arguments
```

And she commits her changes, easy as falling off a greasy log.

```
trunk sally$ svn commit -m "use strtol. atoi is deprecated."
Sending        trunk/pb.c
Transmitting file data .
Committed revision 12.
```

After this commit is finished, Subversion removes her lock so that others can once again modify the file.

10. Tag

Still mourning the loss of his email code, Harry creates a tag so he can more easily access it later.

```
lottery harry$ mkdir tags

lottery harry$ svn add tags
A         tags
```

> Subversion implements *tag* through the use of its "cheap copy" mechanism, which is also used for **branch**. The idea is that Subversion can make a copy of any object in the tree without duplicating all the data. The new copy is simply a link to the other one, but as the two items change, they diverge while sharing their history. In Subversion, a tag is a branch which nobody intends to modify.

```
lottery harry$ svn copy --revision=10 trunk \
                              tags/just_before_sally_deleted_my_email_code

lottery harry$ svn st
A       tags
A  +    tags/just_before_sally_deleted_my_email_code

lottery harry$ svn commit -m "tag snapshot in case I need the email code"
Adding          tags
Adding          tags/just_before_sally_deleted_my_email_code

Committed revision 13.
```

Sally sees Harry gloating in the company chat room about his beloved tag, so she does an update.

```
trunk sally$ svn update
At revision 13.
```

She doesn't get the tag. But Sally didn't just fall off the turnip truck. She notices that she executed that command from the trunk directory. She needs to cd up one level and try again.

> *Note that with Subversion, most commands take effect from the current directory and recurse down. Everything else is ignored. This contrasts with some other VCS tools where most commands work on the entire tree.*

```
trunk sally$ cd ..

lottery sally$ svn update
A    tags
A    tags/just_before_sally_deleted_my_email_code
...
Updated to revision 13.
```

Sally sees Harry's tag and rolls her eyes. Fine. Whatever.

11. Branch

Sally wants more privacy. She decides to create her own branch.

```
lottery sally$ ls
branches    tags         trunk

lottery sally$ svn copy trunk branches/no_boys_allowed
A           branches/no_boys_allowed

lottery sally$ svn st
?           trunk/pb
A  +        branches/no_boys_allowed
?           branches/no_boys_allowed/pb
```

```
lottery sally$ svn commit -m "a private branch so I can work without harry"
Adding          branches/no_boys_allowed

Committed revision 14.
```

Subversion uses directory branches—a branch shows up in the tree as a directory. DVCS tools use a very different branching model. Some people find directory branches easier because they're more visible. One problem with directory branches is that it is possible to commit to two branches at the same time.

Now that Sally is working in her own branch, she feels much more productive. She adds support for the "favorite" option. When a user is playing his favorite numbers, his chances of winning should be doubled. In doing this, she had to rework the way command-line args are parsed. And she removes an atoi() call she missed last time. And she restructures all the error checking into one place.

So main() now looks like this:

```
int main(int argc, char** argv)
{
    int balls[6];
    int count_balls = 0;
    int favorite = 0;

    for (int i=1; i<argc; i++)
    {
        const char* arg = argv[i];

        if ('-' == arg[0])
        {
            if (0 == strcmp(arg, "-favorite"))
            {
                favorite = 1;
            }
            else
            {
                goto usage_error;
            }
        }
        else
```

```
        {
            char* endptr = NULL;
            long val = strtol(arg, &endptr, 10);
            if (*endptr)
            {
                goto usage_error;
            }
            balls[count_balls++] = (int) val;
        }
    }

    if (6 != count_balls)
    {
        goto usage_error;
    }

    int power_ball = balls[5];

    int result = calculate_result(balls, power_ball);

    if (result < 0)
    {
        goto usage_error;
    }

    if (LUCKY_NUMBER == power_ball)
    {
        result = result * 2;
    }

    if (favorite)
    {
        result = result * 2;
    }

    printf("%d percent chance of winning\n", result);

    return 0;

usage_error:
    fprintf(stderr, "Usage: %s [-favorite] (5 white balls) power_ball\n", argv[0]);
    return -1;
}
```

She commits her changes, knowing that the commit will succeed because she is working in her private branch.

```
no_boys_allowed sally$ svn commit -m "add -favorite and cleanup some other stuff"
Sending        no_boys_allowed/pb.c
Transmitting file data .
Committed revision 15.
```

> *I am happy for Sally and her burst of productivity here, but she probably should have made these changes in two or three separate commits instead of squashing them all into one.*

12. Merge (no conflicts)

Meanwhile, over in the trunk, Harry decides the white balls should be sorted before analysing them, because that's how they get shown on the telly.

```
trunk harry$ svn diff
Index: pb.c
===================================================================
--- pb.c    (revision 12)
+++ pb.c    (working copy)
@@ -6,6 +6,25 @@
 #define MAX_WHITE_BALL 59
 #define MAX_POWER_BALL 39

+static int my_sort_func(const void* p1, const void* p2)
+{
+    int v1 = *((int *) p1);
+    int v2 = *((int *) p2);
+
+    if (v1 < v2)
+    {
+        return -1;
+    }
+    else if (v1 > v2)
+    {
+        return 1;
+    }
+    else
+    {
+        return 0;
+    }
+}
+
 int calculate_result(int white_balls[5], int power_ball)
 {
     for (int i=0; i<5; i++)
@@ -27,6 +46,8 @@
         return -1;
     }
```

```
+     qsort(white_balls, 5, sizeof(int), my_sort_func);
+
+     return 0;
}
```

And he commits the change.

```
trunk harry$ svn commit -m "sort the white balls"
Sending        trunk/pb.c
Transmitting file data .
Committed revision 16.
```

But now he's curious about what Sally has been doing. She said he wasn't allowed to commit to her branch but she didn't say anything about **looking** at it.

```
trunk harry$ cd ../branches/

branches harry$ svn update
A    no_boys_allowed
A    no_boys_allowed/pb.c
A    no_boys_allowed/Makefile
Updated to revision 16.

branches harry$ svn log
------------------------------------------------------------------------
r15 | sally | 2011-04-08 09:04:38 -0500 (Fri, 08 Apr 2011) | 1 line

add -favorite and cleanup some other stuff
------------------------------------------------------------------------
...
```

Interesting. She added the "favorite" feature. Harry decides he wants that. So he asks Subversion to merge stuff from Sally's branch into trunk.

```
branches harry$ cd ..

lottery harry$ cd trunk

trunk harry$ svn merge ../branches/no_boys_allowed
--- Merging r14 through r16 into '.':
U    pb.c
```

Smashing! Harry examines pb.c and discovers that it was merged correctly. Sally's "favorite" changes are there and his qsort changes are as well. So he compiles the code, runs a quick test, and commits the merge.

```
trunk harry$ make
gcc -std=c99 -Wall -Wextra -Werror pb.c -o pb

trunk harry$ ./pb -favorite 5 3 33 22 7 31
0 percent chance of winning

trunk harry$ svn commit -m "merge changes from sally"
Sending         trunk
Sending         trunk/pb.c
Transmitting file data .
Committed revision 17.
```

13. Merge (repeated, no conflicts)

Simultaneously, both Harry and Sally realize that their code has no comments.

Harry:

```
trunk harry$ svn diff
Index: pb.c
===================================================================
--- pb.c    (revision 17)
+++ pb.c    (working copy)
@@ -47,6 +47,7 @@
        return -1;
    }

+    // lottery ball numbers are always shown sorted
    qsort(white_balls, 5, sizeof(int), my_sort_func);

    return 0;

trunk harry$ svn commit -m "just a comment"
Sending         trunk/pb.c
Transmitting file data .
Committed revision 18.
```

And Sally:

```
no_boys_allowed sally$ svn diff
Index: pb.c
===================================================================
--- pb.c    (revision 15)
+++ pb.c    (working copy)
@@ -35,7 +35,7 @@
  {
      int balls[6];
      int count_balls = 0;
-     int favorite = 0;
```

```
+    int favorite = 0;  // this should be a bool

     for (int i=1; i<argc; i++)
     {
@@ -69,10 +69,13 @@
         goto usage_error;
     }

+    // the power ball is always the last one given
     int power_ball = balls[5];

     int result = calculate_result(balls, power_ball);

+    // calculate result can return -1 if the ball numbers
+    // are out of range
     if (result < 0)
     {
         goto usage_error;
no_boys_allowed sally$ svn commit -m "a few comments"
Sending        no_boys_allowed/pb.c
Transmitting file data .
Committed revision 19.
```

Harry decides to try again to merge the changes from Sally's branch.

Subversion does a nice job with the repeated merge here. On the first merge, it gets r14 through r16. On this second merge, it gets r17 through r19, because it remembered the previous merge.

```
lottery harry$ svn update
U    branches/no_boys_allowed/pb.c
Updated to revision 19.

lottery harry$ cd trunk

trunk harry$ svn merge ../branches/no_boys_allowed/
--- Merging r17 through r19 into '.':
U    pb.c

trunk harry$ svn diff

Property changes on: .
_____
Modified: svn:mergeinfo
```

```
   Merged /branches/no_boys_allowed:r17-19

Index: pb.c
===================================================================
--- pb.c      (revision 19)
+++ pb.c      (working copy)
@@ -57,7 +57,7 @@
 {
     int balls[6];
     int count_balls = 0;
-    int favorite = 0;
+    int favorite = 0;   // this should be a bool

     for (int i=1; i<argc; i++)
     {
@@ -91,10 +91,13 @@
         goto usage_error;
     }

+    // the power ball is always the last one given
     int power_ball = balls[5];

     int result = calculate_result(balls, power_ball);

+    // calculate result can return -1 if the ball numbers
+    // are out of range
     if (result < 0)
     {
         goto usage_error;
```

No worries on the merge then. Harry checks to see if everything compiles, and commits the merge.

```
trunk harry$ make
gcc -std=c99 -Wall -Wextra -Werror pb.c -o pb

trunk harry$ svn commit -m "merge changes from sally"
Sending        trunk
Sending        trunk/pb.c
Transmitting file data .
Committed revision 20.
```

14. Merge (conflicts)

Sally realizes that C99 has a bool type that should have been used.

```
no_boys_allowed sally$ svn diff
Index: pb.c
===================================================================
--- pb.c      (revision 19)
```

```
+++ pb.c     (working copy)
@@ -2,6 +2,7 @@
 #include <stdio.h>
 #include <stdlib.h>
 #include <string.h>
+#include <stdbool.h>

 #define LUCKY_NUMBER 7
 #define MAX_WHITE_BALL 59
@@ -35,7 +36,7 @@
 {
     int balls[6];
     int count_balls = 0;
-    int favorite = 0;   // this should be a bool
+    bool favorite = false;

     for (int i=1; i<argc; i++)
     {
@@ -45,7 +46,7 @@
         {
             if (0 == strcmp(arg, "-favorite"))
             {
-                favorite = 1;
+                favorite = true;
             }
             else
             {

no_boys_allowed sally$ svn commit -m "use the bool type"
Sending        no_boys_allowed/pb.c
Transmitting file data .
Committed revision 21.
```

Meanwhile, Harry has been grumbling about Sally's butchering of the Queen's English and decides to correct the spelling of the word "favourite".

```
trunk harry$ svn diff
Index: pb.c
========================================================================
--- pb.c     (revision 20)
+++ pb.c     (working copy)
@@ -57,7 +57,7 @@
 {
     int balls[6];
     int count_balls = 0;
-    int favorite = 0;  // this should be a bool
+    int favourite = 0;  // this should be a bool

     for (int i=1; i<argc; i++)
     {
@@ -65,9 +65,9 @@

         if ('-' == arg[0])
```

```
        {
-           if (0 == strcmp(arg, "-favorite"))
+           if (0 == strcmp(arg, "-favourite"))
            {
-               favorite = 1;
+               favourite = 1;
            }
            else
            {
@@ -108,7 +108,7 @@
            result = result * 2;
        }

-       if (favorite)
+       if (favourite)
        {
            result = result * 2;
        }
@@ -118,7 +118,7 @@
        return 0;

 usage_error:
-       fprintf(stderr, "Usage: %s [-favorite] (5 white balls) power_ball\n", argv[0]);
+       fprintf(stderr, "Usage: %s [-favourite] (5 white balls) power_ball\n", argv[0]);
        return -1;
 }
```

Feeling quite chuffed about his pedantry, Harry proceeds to commit the change.

```
trunk harry$ svn commit -m "fixed spelling error"
Sending          trunk/pb.c
Transmitting file data .
Committed revision 22.
```

And to once again merge Sally's changes into trunk.

```
trunk harry$ cd ..

lottery harry$ svn update
U    branches/no_boys_allowed/pb.c
Updated to revision 22.

lottery harry$ cd trunk

trunk harry$ svn merge ../branches/no_boys_allowed/
Conflict discovered in 'pb.c'.
Select: (p) postpone, (df) diff-full, (e) edit,
        (mc) mine-conflict, (tc) theirs-conflict,
        (s) show all options:
```

Crikey! Conflicts in pb.c again.

```
trunk harry$ svn diff
Index: pb.c
================================================================
--- pb.c     (revision 22)
+++ pb.c     (working copy)
@@ -2,6 +2,7 @@
 #include <stdio.h>
 #include <stdlib.h>
 #include <string.h>
+#include <stdbool.h>

 #define LUCKY_NUMBER 7
 #define MAX_WHITE_BALL 59
@@ -57,7 +58,11 @@
 {
     int balls[6];
     int count_balls = 0;
+<<<<<<< .working
     int favourite = 0;  // this should be a bool
+=======
+    bool favorite = false;
+>>>>>>> .merge-right.r22

     for (int i=1; i<argc; i++)
     {
@@ -67,7 +72,11 @@
         {
             if (0 == strcmp(arg, "-favourite"))
             {
+<<<<<<< .working
                 favourite = 1;
+=======
+                favorite = true;
+>>>>>>> .merge-right.r22
             }
             else
             {
```

Now this **is** a sticky wicket! Harry quickly realises this conflict needs to be resolved manually by keeping the proper spelling but converting the type to bool like Sally did.

```
trunk harry$ svn diff

Property changes on: .
_____
Modified: svn:mergeinfo
   Merged /branches/no_boys_allowed:r20-22

Index: pb.c
================================================================
--- pb.c     (revision 22)
+++ pb.c     (working copy)
@@ -2,6 +2,7 @@
```

```
 #include <stdio.h>
 #include <stdlib.h>
 #include <string.h>
+#include <stdbool.h>

 #define LUCKY_NUMBER 7
 #define MAX_WHITE_BALL 59
@@ -57,7 +58,7 @@
 {
     int balls[6];
     int count_balls = 0;
-    int favourite = 0;  // this should be a bool
+    bool favourite = false;

     for (int i=1; i<argc; i++)
     {
@@ -67,7 +68,7 @@
         {
             if (0 == strcmp(arg, "-favourite"))
             {
-                favourite = 1;
+                favourite = true;
             }
             else
             {
```

After manually merging the changes, Harry proceeds to resolve the conflict and commit the merge.

```
trunk harry$ svn resolve --accept=working pb.c
Resolved conflicted state of 'pb.c'

trunk harry$ svn commit -m "merge, conflicts fixed"
Sending        trunk
Sending        trunk/pb.c
Transmitting file data .
Committed revision 23.
```

And all of Futilisoft's customers lived happily ever after.

15. Summary

The following table summarizes all 18 commands for Subversion. See Table A.1 in Appendix A for a comparison of Subversion's commands with other tools.

Operation	Subversion Command
Create	svnadmin create
Checkout	svn checkout
Commit	svn commit
Update	svn update
Add	svn add
Edit	[a]
Delete	svn delete
Rename	svn move
Move	svn move
Status	svn status
Diff	svn diff
Revert	svn revert
Log	svn log
Tag	svn copy[b]
Branch	svn copy[c]
Merge	svn merge
Resolve	svn resolve
Lock	svn lock

[a]Automatic: Subversion will notice that the file has changed.

[b]Built on Subversion's "cheap copy" mechanism. Appears as a directory in the tree. Equivalent to a branch that never gets modified.

[c]Built on Subversion's "cheap copy" mechanism. Appears as a directory in the tree.

2

Distributed Version Control

More Basics

Third generation version control tools operate in a manner we could describe as *distributed* or *decentralized*. These DVCS tools build upon the same concepts we discussed in Chapter 2, but there are some additional nouns and three new verbs (for a total of 21) we need to define.

1. Clone

Create a new repository instance that is a copy of another.

The essential difference between a Centralized Version Control System (CVCS) and a DVCS is the notion of a *repository instance*.

Just like with a CVCS, when a repository is created for the very first time, we use **create**. After that, what makes a DVCS different is that we can have multiple instances of that repository. The **clone** operation is the way those new instances get created.

In a CVCS, the repository exists in one place on a central server. Every piece of software that is used to access the repository includes a network client. See Figure 4.1.

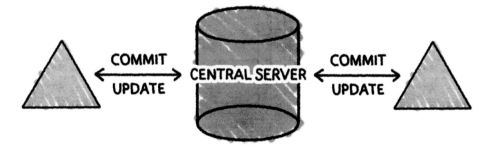

Figure 4.1. Centralized Version Control

In contrast, a DVCS allows the repository to exist in more than one place. We can have multiple repository instances. Of course, having more than one instance of the repository means that we will need ways of keeping them synchronized.

In fact, not only does a DVCS **allow** multiple repository instances, it generally works that way all the time. Most operations interact with a local repository instance, not a network server. The only time networking code gets involved is when the repository instances are being synchronized. Every developer has his own private repository instance. The typical situation ends up looking like Figure 4.2.

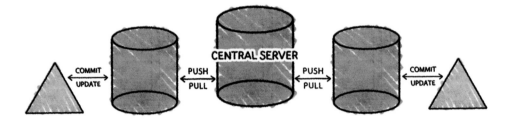

Figure 4.2. Decentralized Version Control

Upon someone's first exposure to the DVCS concept, it is common to hear them express a measure of alarm because they think that there will not be a central server. But this worry is not necessary. The point of multiple repository instances is not to eliminate the central server. Rather, the point is to get more flexibility. With a CVCS, the central server is the only repository instance, so it must do everything. With a DVCS, we can have repository instances that are dedicated to specific purposes.

In practice, virtually all DVCS teams have a central server. With a CVCS, a central server happens because it is inherent in the centralized model. With a DVCS, a central server happens because of the team's decision to have one.

2. Push
Copy changesets from a local repository instance to a remote one.

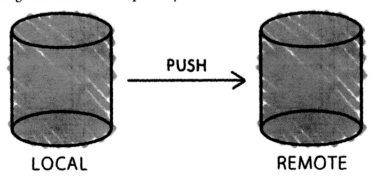

The **push** operation is used for synchronization between two repository instances. Specifically, this operation happens from the perspective of a local repository instance that wants to copy some changesets into a remote instance. Usually, the remote instance is the one from which the local instance was originally cloned.

Note that the two repository instances are not necessarily identical after the push. We may have constrained the push by instructing the VCS to only send some of the local changes. Or the remote instance may contain things that are not in the local instance.

3. Pull

Copy changesets from a remote repository instance to a local one.

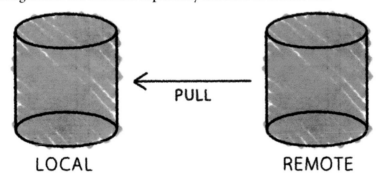

The **pull** operation is also used for synchronization between two repository instances. Specifically, this operation happens from the perspective of a local repository instance that wants to copy some changesets from a remote repository instance. Usually, the remote instance is the one from which the local instance was originally cloned.

Note that the two repository instances are not necessarily identical after the pull. We may have constrained the pull (by instructing the VCS to only pull some of the remote changes). Or the local instance may contain things that are not in the remote instance. In order to completely synchronize two instances, you would have to pull everything from the remote instance and then push everything from the local instance.

4. Directed Acyclic Graphs (DAGs)

In order to support the ability to push and pull changesets between multiple instances of the same repository, we need a specially designed structure for representing multiple versions of things. The structure we use is called a Directed Acyclic Graph (DAG), a design which is more expressive than a purely linear model. The history of everything in the repository is modeled as a DAG.

Second generation tools tend to model the history of a repository as a line. The linear history model is tried and true. History is a sequence of versions, one after the other, as shown in Figure 4.3.

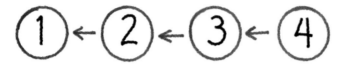

Figure 4.3. Repository History as a Line

To create a new version:

1. Grab the latest version
2. Make some changes to it
3. Check it back in

People like linear history for its simplicity. It provides an unambiguous answer to the question of which version is latest.

But the linear model has one big problem: You can only commit a new version if it was based on the latest version. And this kind of thing happens a lot:

+ I grab the latest version. At the time I grabbed it, this was version 3.
+ I make some changes to it.
+ While I am doing this, somebody commits version 4.
+ When I go to commit my changes, I can't, because they are not based on the repository's current version. The parent for my changes was version 3 because that's what was current when I started.

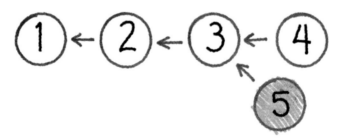

Figure 4.4. Not a Line

The linear model of history won't allow me to create version 5 as shown in Figure 4.4. Instead, a linear history VCS requires me to take the changes which were made between versions 3 and 4 and apply them to my version. The result is that my working copy's parent gets changed from 3 to 4, thus allowing me to commit.

This is unfortunate. My changes were made against version 3, but now they are getting blended with the changes from version 4. What if they don't blend well?

The obvious question is: What would happen if we allowed 5 to be checked in with 3 as its parent? Our history would no longer be a line. Instead it would be a Directed Acyclic Graph (DAG).

A DAG is a data structure from computer science which can be used to model a wide variety of problems. The DAG consists of the following elements:

+ Nodes. Each node represents some object or piece of data. In the case of a DVCS, each node represents one revision of the entire repository tree.

+ Directed edges. A directed edge (or "arrow") from one node to another represents some kind of relationship between those two nodes. In our situation, the arrow means "is based on". By convention, I draw DAG arrows from child to parent, from the new revision to the revision from which it was derived. Arrows in a DAG may not form a cycle.

+ A root node. At least one of the nodes will have no parents. This is the root of the DAG.

+ Leaf nodes. One or more of the nodes will have no children. These are called leaves or leaf nodes.

A major feature of the DAG model for history is that it doesn't interrupt the developer at the moment she is trying to commit her work. In this fashion, the DAG is probably a more pure representation of what happens in a team practicing concurrent development. Version 5 was in fact based on version 3, so why not just represent that fact?

Well, it turns out there is a darn good reason why not. In the DAG above, we don't know which version is "the latest". This causes all kinds of problems:

+ Suppose we need the changes in versions 4 and 5 in order to ship our release. Currently we can't have that. There is no version in the system that includes both.

+ Our build system is configured to always build the latest version. What is it supposed to do now?

+ Even if we build both 4 and 5, which one is QA supposed to test?

- If a developer wants to update her working copy to the latest version, which one is it? When a developer wants to make some changes, which version should he use as the baseline?

- Our project manager wants to know which tasks are done and how much work is left to do. His notion of "done" is very closely associated with the concept of "latest". If he can't figure out which version is latest, his brain is likely to just blue screen when he tries to update the Gantt chart.

Yep, this is a bad scene. Civilization as we know it will probably just shut down.

In order to avoid dogs and cats living together with mass hysteria, the tools that use a DAG model of history provide a way to resolve the mess. The answer is the same as it is with linear history. We need a merge. But instead of requiring the developer to merge before committing, we allow that merge to happen later.

Somebody needs to construct a version which contains all the changes in both version 4 and version 5. When this version gets committed, it will have arrows pointing to both of its "parents" as shown by version 6 in Figure 4.5.

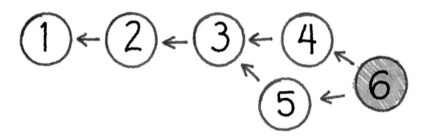

Figure 4.5. Sort of like a Line

Order has been restored. Once again we know which version is "the latest". If somebody bothers to reboot the project manager, he will probably realize that this DAG looks almost like a line. Except for that weird stuff happening between versions 3 and 6, it is a line. Best not to lose sleep over it.

What this project manager doesn't know is that this particular crisis was minor. He thinks that his paradigm has been completely challenged, but one day he's going to come into his office and find something like the picture in Figure 4.6.

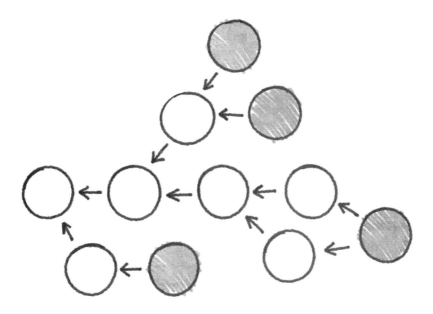

Figure 4.6. Not even close to being a Line

Now what? If you're living in the linear history paradigm, this DAG is an absolute disaster. It has **four** leaf nodes. Everything that needs to know which version is latest is about to completely fall apart, including the aforementioned product manager who is probably now in his office curled up in a fetal position and hoping that Mommy included cookies with his SpaghettiOs for lunch.

The linear history model is looking pretty good right now. There's a good reason why 99.44% of developers are using a version control tool built on the notion of history as a line. (Yes, I made that statistic up.)

And yet, despite all this apparent chaos, we should remind ourselves of the primary benefit of the DAG model: It more accurately describes the way developers work. It doesn't make developers bend to its will like the linear model does. When a developer wants to check something in, she does, and the DAG merely records what happened.

Many teams will always prefer the linear history model, even if it requires them to make their development process compatible with it, and there's nothing wrong with that. Life is simpler that way.

But the DAG model is more flexible and expressive, and many teams can benefit from a VCS which has those qualities.

And for other teams, the DAG model might be coming along simply because they want to use a DVCS tool for other reasons. DVCS tools use a DAG because they have to. If we can't assume a live connection to a central server, there isn't any way to force developers to make everything fit into the linear model.

So we need to figure out ways of coping with the DAG. How do we do this?

One way is to reframe every operation. If you tell a doctor that "it hurts when I need to know which version is latest", the doctor will tell you to "stop doing that". Instead, always specify exactly which node to use:

- The build machine doesn't build the latest node. Instead, it builds whichever node we tell it to build. Or maybe it builds every node.

- QA tests whichever build somebody decides they should test.

- Developers don't update their tree to "the latest". Instead, they look at the DAG, pick a node, and update to that one.

I'm not saying this approach is always practical. I am merely observing that it is conceptually valid. If you want your DAG to have multiple leaf nodes, you can do that. As long as you're willing to specify which node you want to use, any operation that needs a node can proceed.

In practice, the most common solution to this problem is to have stricter rules about the shape of the DAG on the central server. In other words, developers are allowed to have all manner of DAG chaos in their private repository instances, but the DAG on the central server must have a single leaf node.

Typically, a DVCS will warn you if you are attempting a push which would make the remote repository's DAG messy. Users of Mercurial and Veracity would typically handle this situation by doing a pull, then a merge, and then retrying the push.

Git users often handle this situation differently, using Git's *rebase* feature. Rebase is a way of rewriting changesets, replacing them with new ones that are exactly equivalent but which have different parents. The way this feature is typically used is to rewrite DAG history as a line. In other words, even though Git is clearly a third generation version control tool, many of its users prefer the cleaner, linear history of a second generation tool.

Because Git's rebase command alters things which have already been committed to a repository instance, it often serves as a launching point for arguments among DVCS fans with different perspectives on the immutability of a repository instance.

One final note about DAGs: It would be conceptually valid to use the notion of a DAG to discuss the divergence of any part of a repository. However, when we speak of a DAG with respect to a DVCS, we're talking about the whole tree. This is how branching works in DVCS land—each node of the DAG is a version of the whole tree. This contrasts with CVCS tools where most popular implementations model a branch as a directory in the tree which was branched from another directory in the tree.

5   Advantages

With obvious exceptions like furniture and Star Wars movies, new things tend to be better than old things. The state of the art advances. An industry's more recent offerings usually incorporate better technology and practices.

The reason DVCS tools are the third generation of version control is that they are in several ways better than the second generation offerings. In this chapter I will discuss some of the advantages a DVCS can provide over the centralized tools.

1. Private Workspace

The concept of a private workspace is central to **all** version control tools. Centralized version control systems provide developers with a private place to work by giving them a working copy. A DVCS takes this one step further by giving them a private copy of the whole repository.

Why is the notion of a private workspace so important?

Table 5.1. Lines of Communication

People	1	4	10
Lines	None	6	45

The most productive developer is alone. A solitary developer never has to worry about coordinating with anyone else. But as soon as the project goes plural, there is overhead.[1] And for every developer added to the team, the overhead gets worse.[2]

It is the job of the VCS to help manage this overhead and minimize the effects. The primary way it achieves this goal is to give the developer the ability to pretend, for a little while, that he is the only member of the team. The VCS provides a private workspace.

Once again, this concept is similar to multi-threaded programming, where we get maximum performance when we avoid thread synchronization as much as possible. A thread can get a lot of work done during the times when it doesn't have to wait on other threads. The thread can pretend, for a little while, that it is the only thread in its process.

By giving developers a private copy of the entire repository, the DVCS opens up much more flexibility for the kind of things they can do in their private workspace. Instead of just editing files in the working copy, developers can use all 18 of the basic verbs (see Chapter 2).

For example, a developer using a DVCS can commit as often she wants. The act of committing a change to a repository instance is distinct from the act of publishing that change to the rest of the team. The developer can pretend, for a little while, that she is the only person on the team, deferring the overhead of coordination with others until she is ready to push her work to the central server.

2. Fast

Developers usually don't realize how fast a DVCS can be until they've tried one—stuff is really, really fast when most of your operations are against a local repository instance instead of a server. For example, I just ran a quick test where I committed the entire valgrind[3] tree (3,143 files; total size 42 MB) using Subversion and several DVCS tools. The timing results in Table 5.2 show that Subversion is **way** slower than the DVCS crowd. Broadly speaking, developers who switch from [almost] any CVCS to [almost] any DVCS experience performance gains like these for [almost] all daily operations.

---

[1]It seems wrong to discuss this concept without mentioning "The Mythical Man-Month", a classic book on software engineering by Fred Brooks.
[2]The function is n*(n-1)/2.
[3]http://www.valgrind.org/

Table 5.2. Ridiculously Unscientific Benchmarks

Operation	Subversion (svnserve on 127.0.0.1)	Bazaar	Mercurial	Veracity	Git
Commit	21.9 s	5.2 s	4.6 s	3.7 s	3.2 s[a]

[a]Nobody ever talks about Git winning any awards for ease of use, but good gracious, it is fast.

3. Offline

When talking about disconnected operation, the so-called "airplane example" is invariably the first thing talked about. Stop me if you've heard this one, but a developer has to fly across the country and writes some code on the plane. Two hours in, at 31,000 feet, he's finished his changes and wants to commit them. With a DVCS, this is possible, since he has a repository instance on his laptop. How cool is that?!?!?

Well, not really that cool, if we're honest. When it comes right down to it, most programmers don't fly on airplanes very much. When they do fly on airplanes, they use their laptops to watch Han Solo get frozen in carbonite for the 73rd time, not to write code. If, by some chance, they do write some code on the plane, it's not always true that they actually **need** to commit the changes. Finally, in 2011, many commercial airlines are offering in-flight Wi-Fi. Conclusion: Airplanes are not the best metaphor to use when talking about working while disconnected.

The thing I hate most about the metaphor is not its fundamental dumbness (though I do hate that plenty), but that disconnected operation is an important benefit of a DVCS and the airplane example is a lousy way to convince anyone of that fact.

Why does disconnected operation matter? Here's one simple scenario: Suppose you are offline and you want to fix two unrelated bugs and commit them in separate changesets. With a second generation tool, you can't commit until you get back online, so both of the bug-fixes are going to end up in your pending changeset at the same time.

Fine, so a DVCS is great when you're offline. But that never happens anymore, right?

Actually, it does. If you need Internet access all the time, you will quickly discover how often you don't have it.

I find that Wi-Fi Internet access is like the police. It's everywhere… except when you really need it. Everywhere I go, I see cafes with Wi-Fi signs and McDonald's with Wi-Fi signs and I have a laptop, an iPad, and an Android phone that all support Wi-Fi but I still have the strong impression that when I really need to use Wi-Fi, it's not there.

This very paragraph is being written at 12:45pm on April 15th, 2011. I am sitting in the food court at the mall in Champaign, Illinois. There is no Wi-Fi here.

Furthermore, just because I have **some** form of connectivity does not mean that I want to be dependent on it. Even more common than "no Wi-Fi" is "crappy Wi-Fi" with high latency and packet loss. There are good reasons why I may want to do stuff offline and then sync. Peter Deutsch wrote about his "fallacies of distributed computing"[4] back in 1994, and they still apply.

We've never had more Internet than we have right now, and we still don't have enough. There may come a time when offline operation is no longer an important part of the DVCS story, but that time is not yet here.

4. Geography

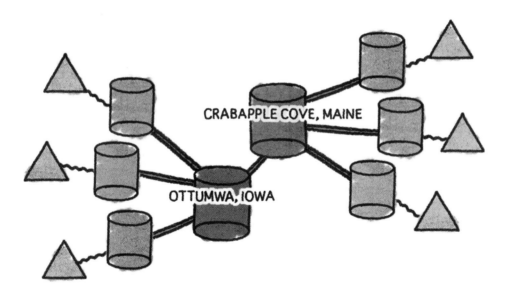

Figure 5.1. Geographically Distributed Teams

Consider a development team that is split up in two cities. Half the team is in a satellite office in Crabapple Cove, Maine, and the other half is at the company's headquarters in Ottumwa, Iowa. With a CVCS, they have to pick one city to hold the central server and everybody in the other city has to access it over an Internet link. With a DVCS (as

---

[4]http://en.wikipedia.org/wiki/Fallacies_of_Distributed_Computing

shown in Figure 5.1), they can set up a central server in each city and use push and pull to synchronize them whenever as they want.

5. Flexible Workflows

Geography isn't the only reason you might want to have more than one central server. You might also want to create a repository instance to support a specific purpose. Or you might want to use named branches to manage simultaneous work on more than one release. Bottom line: A DVCS offers incredible flexibility to support any kind of workflow your team needs. See Chapter 11 for more information.

6. Easier Merging

Branching is easy. Merging is hard.

Branching is like two people going off in their own directions and not collaborating. What's hard about that?

If you think about it, in nature divergence is easier than convergence. Literal trees (like oak and maple) branch but they don't merge. When a family enters Disney's Magic Kingdom theme park, they can all run off and do their own thing, or they can spend half an hour bickering over which section of the park to see first.

People using a CVCS tend to avoid branching because most of those centralized tools aren't very good at merging. When they switch to a DVCS, they tend to bring that attitude with them, even though it's not really necessary anymore. Decentralized tools are much better at merging.

Why are they better?

+ They're built on a DAG (see Section 4 in Chapter 4). Merge algorithms need good information about history and common ancestors. A DAG is a better way to represent that kind of information than the techniques used by most centralized tools.

+ They keep the developer's intended changes distinct from the merge she had to do in order to get those changes committed. This approach is less error-prone at commit time, since the developer's changes are already cleanly tucked away in an immutable changeset. The only thing that needs to be done is the merge itself, so it gets all the attention it needs. Later, when tracking down a problem, it is easy to figure out if the problem happened during the intended changes or the merge, since those two things are distinct in the history.

+ They deal with *whole-tree branches*, not directory branches. The path names in the tree are independent of the branch. This improves interoperability with other tooling.

7. Implicit Backup

Perhaps I shouldn't use the word "backup" here. I certainly do not mean to imply that using a DVCS means you don't need to have a backup strategy.

But the central principle of any backup strategy is that your chances of losing data go down when you have more copies of it. Some folks (including me) do feel better about their version control data when using a DVCS because there are multiple instances of the repository. At SourceGear we have a central server with RAID and ECC RAM and redundant power supplies and regular backups with offsite storage and stuff like that. But we get a little extra security knowing that there are dozens more live copies of the whole repository regularly being used on other machines. Any of them could become the central repository on short notice.

8. Scale out, not just up

With a CVCS, the server holding the central repository needs to be powerful enough to serve the needs of the entire team. For a team of 10 people, this is not an issue. For larger teams, the hardware limitations of the server can be a performance bottleneck.

Some systems (such as IBM Rational ClearCase or Microsoft Team Foundation Server) expect the server to do a **lot** of work. It can be challenging and expensive to set up a server to support thousands of users.

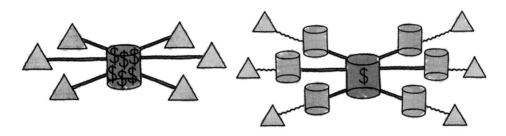

Generally speaking, a DVCS has much more modest hardware requirements for a central server. Users don't interact with the server unless they need to push or pull. All the heavy lifting happens on the client side so the server hardware can be very simple indeed.

With a DVCS, it is also possible to scale the central server by turning it into a server farm. Instead of one large server machine, you can add capacity by adding more small server machines, using scripts to keep them all in sync with each other.

6 Weaknesses

It's not **all** pretty flowers and frolicking deer for DVCS systems; there are a few areas where solutions from the CVCS world still win.

Before I begin, let me say a word about the freshness date of the material in this chapter. As I write this in mid-2011, the most popular tools in the DVCS world are Git, Mercurial, and Bazaar. The issues mentioned here are common legitimate criticisms heard by CVCS users who are evaluating the decentralized model for version control. But things are moving very fast.

- Git, Mercurial, and Bazaar all remain under active development by very smart people. New and improved versions are coming out regularly.
- Relatively recent tools like Fossil[1] are bringing new ideas.
- All the established CVCS leaders are searching for ways to morph their products into a DVCS, or least into some kind of hybrid. Nobody knows yet if or when one of these companies will find a sweet spot, a CVCS which brings just enough benefits from the DVCS architecture.
- In the design and implementation of Veracity, some of the issues in this chapter have been particular areas of focus for us, areas where we want Veracity to go further than previously available solutions.

So the version control arena is in a sea of change right now, but I am confident of two things:

1. DVCS is the way of the future for version control. This model **will** become mainstream.
2. In the DVCS world, the current state of the art is just the beginning.

---

[1] http://www.fossil-scm.org/

1. Locks

Just as I believe that many software teams should use **lock** rarely or never, I also understand that for some, **lock** is a critical feature. A great example is a team building a game with lots of graphical assets kept under version control along with the code. With binary files and other cases where automerge cannot work, locking a file is often the right way to go.

For somewhat obvious reasons, there isn't much support for **lock** in distributed version control. When the system is designed to provide excellent support for offline usage, a feature which requires online usage is not likely to get much focus. Unless and until DVCS tools provide support for **lock**, gaming companies are probably going to stay with centralized tools.

2. Very Large Repositories

Having the whole repository on your laptop is fine if it's a gigabyte. If it's a **terabyte**, not so much.

The issue isn't really disk space. Disk space is as cheap as it's ever been and still getting cheaper. The problem is network speed. If the initial clone involves moving 1 TB onto your desktop machine, it's gonna take a while.

The current best practice with a DVCS is to break things up into smaller repositories. If you have a single repository that is more than a terabyte in size and absolutely cannot be broken up into smaller ones, then you have many, many problems. One of those problems is that it will not be feasible for you to use a DVCS.

3. Integration

Industry-wide, there has been a trend toward more integration between version control and other stuff like project tracking, wikis, discussion forums, build management, etc. Developers don't just commit code. They use a whole bunch of other tools which help them collaborate with each other and with people in other functional areas. The expectation is that all these tools will integrate together very well, providing a seamless user experience. This concept is sometimes referred to as Application Lifecycle Management (ALM).

The rapidly increasing popularity of DVCS is generating some momentum in the opposite direction. The benefits of a DVCS (such as offline usage) are somewhat diminished if all of the other tools a developer needs are still centralized.

Yes, it's cool that I can commit my code while I'm on a yacht[2], but how do I update the bug tracking system to mark the bug fixed? So far, the answer is that I have to wait until the boat gets to shore, hope that the port terminal has Wi-Fi, log in to my corporate VPN, bring up a web browser, remember the bug ID, find the bug, change its status, and try to remember my code changes so I can write something relevant in the comments. That's not what I want. What I want is to do all those things offline to my local clone of the bug tracking database and those changes will get pushed at the same time that I push the version control stuff.

4. Obliterate

The "Implicit Backup" idea described in the previous chapter is a coin with two sides. Having lots of copies of the data does reduce the risk of losing that data, but it also makes it far more difficult to destroy.

Some version control systems have a way of actually altering the history of the repository. There are certain legitimate situations where we want to delete something and have it actually be deleted. In general, these situations arise when someone has a legal obligation to destroy all copies of some piece of data. It is insufficient to use the **delete** operation, since that doesn't purge the data from the repository's history. This feature is commonly known as "obliterate".

Most version control tools do not support obliterate. It is generally agreed that the most important trait for a VCS is reliability. In the pursuit of reliability, anything which allows the history of a repository to be altered is at best a distraction and at worst, damaging. In many cases, any provision for the ability to obliterate things would cause the overall

---

[2]Certain comments from early reviewers of this book motivate me to clarify that I do **not** actually have a yacht.

design to be altered in ways that compromise the performance and reliability of all operations.

As you can tell, I don't like obliterate much. My company has been selling version control tools for over a decade, and our experience in providing technical support to our customers shows that obliterate is often misused. In my entire career, I don't think I've ever found occasion to use obliterate. But I concede that there are valid use cases for it, and the presence of multiple repository instances does make things more difficult, so I mention it here.

With a DVCS, obliterating something would look roughly like this:

- Get one repository instance Q which is complete. You'll need to have every repository instance push everything to Q.

- Clone Q while excluding the parts you want to obliterate. This requires that your DVCS support some kind of a "clone with exclude" operation.

- Destroy all repository instances, replacing them with the clone you just created.

The difficulty of this recipe is determined primarily by the number of repository instances you have. With 10 instances, it's probably not a big problem. With 5,000 instances, you've got a major task on your hands. Fortunately, the need to obliterate is extremely rare.

Or at least it **should** be. If your regular process involves a frequent need to obliterate, you should not be using a DVCS. In fact, my opinion would be that you should not be using **any** VCS in that kind of situation. You're doing something that version control tools are not designed to do. You don't need version control. What you need is something else, something that is not the subject of this book.

5. Administration

A nice thing about a CVCS is that the repository server provides a nice centralized place to do administration, including security, access control, permissions, management of user accounts, etc.

Git and Mercurial are a bit weak in the area of administrative features and user accounts. Both of these tools allow the user to identify himself with any string, and that string is recorded in the repository history.

6. Path-Based Access Control

Decentralized version control tools do not provide a viable way to control access to specific files or directories within the repository tree.

For example, suppose that you want to protect a certain directory by preventing certain users from reading its contents. With a CVCS, most commands operate on part of the repository. Also, the central server is involved with all attempts to read repository data. This model makes it straightforward to control access by repository tree path.

With a DVCS, most commands operate upon the entire repository tree. Furthermore, a complete clone of the repository is already present on the user's machine—there is no secure way of preventing them from reading it.

Users who choose decentralized version control typically must arrange things such that access control on a per-repository basis is sufficient.

7. Ease of Use

Ease of use is a fairly subjective thing, but I include this section here because I believe most people agree that a DVCS is somewhat more difficult to use and understand than a CVCS.

Returning once again to my multi-threaded programming comparison, this is not entirely unexpected. Concurrency is inherently more difficult. Multi-threaded programming is far more challenging than writing code for a single isolated thread.

I've watched many people climb the DVCS learning curve, and they all seem to stumble on the same obstacles.

- How can our team work without a central server? (Answer: You don't have to.)
- With all these repository instances, how do I know which one has the official version of our code? (Answer: Whichever one you designate.)
- How can it be okay to commit changes without merging them first? (Answer: The DVCS remembers the ancestry of your change and allows you to do the merge later.)
- What happened to revision numbers? The version of my tree is e69de29bb2d1d6434b8b29ae775ad8c2e48c5391? What's up with that? (Answer: The DVCS is using cryptographic hashes to store things by content.)

Most people who reach DVCS enlightenment will agree that it was worth the climb.

But it can still make sense for organizations to consider things like training costs as they evaluate a transition. I can't express this any better than Greg Hudson did in his 2004 essay[3] "Undiagnosing Subversion", so I'll just quote him: "In many environments, a shallow learning curve is the most important feature of a version control system."

8. GUIs

There are many software developers who strongly prefer **not** to use a command-line interface. Most of them stopped reading this book several chapters ago.

Like it or not, the command-line nature of this book somewhat reflects current reality in the DVCS world. I'm not saying there are no graphical UIs for the popular DVCS tools. There are plenty of them. But I have the strong impression that distributed version control hasn't got much traction yet among developers that don't use the command line. This will change over time.

---

[3] http://web.mit.edu/ghudson/thoughts/undiagnosing

7 Basics with Mercurial

Futilisoft has begun work on a new product. This product calculates the probability (as an integer percentage) of winning the Powerball for any given set of numbers.

The company has assigned two developers to work on this new project, Harry, located in Birmingham, England, and Sally, located in Birmingham, Alabama. Both developers are telecommuting to the Futilisoft corporate headquarters in Cleveland. After a bit of discussion, they have decided to implement their product as a command-line app in C and to use Mercurial[1] 1.7.3 for version control.

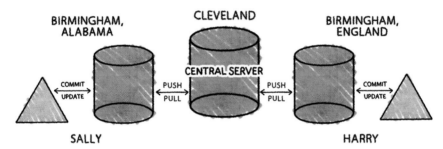

1. Create

Sally gets the project started by creating a new repository.

```
~ server$ mkdir lottery

~ server$ cd lottery

lottery server$ hg init

lottery server$ hg serve
listening at http://server.futilisoft.com:8000/ (bound to *:8000)
```

---

[1]http://mercurial-scm.org/

> *I consider the details of server configuration to be beyond the scope of this book. Please accept my unsubstantiated claim that it happened. Right here.*

2. Clone, Add, Status, Commit

By this time Harry is done dossing about and is ready to start coding.

Since this is Harry's first time using Mercurial, he first sets up his .hgrc file with a user string that will be used to identify his commits in the log.

```
[ui]
username = Harry <harry@futilisoft.com>
```

Now he needs to get his own repository instance.

```
~ harry$ [hg clone] http://server.futilisoft.com:8000/ ./lottery
no changes found
updating to branch default
0 files updated, 0 files merged, 0 files removed, 0 files unresolved
```

> *Note that Mercurial doesn't have a **Checkout** command. It keeps the repository instance within the administrative area of the working copy. This means you can only have one working copy for each repository instance.*

Harry wonders if Sally has already done anything in the new repository.

```
~ harry$ cd lottery

lottery harry$ ls -al
total 0
drwxr-xr-x   3 harry  staff  102 May 17 07:55 .
drwxr-xr-x  21 harry  staff  714 May 17 07:55 ..
drwxr-xr-x   8 harry  staff  272 May 17 07:55 .hg
```

Apparently not. Nothing here but the .hg administrative area. Jolly good then. It's time to start coding. He opens his text editor and creates the starting point for their product.

```c
#include <stdio.h>
#include <stdlib.h>

int calculate_result(int white_balls[5], int power_ball)
{
    return 0;
}

int main(int argc, char** argv)
{
    if (argc != 7)
    {
        fprintf(stderr, "Usage: %s power_ball (5 white balls)\n", argv[0]);
        return -1;
    }

    int power_ball = atoi(argv[1]);

    int white_balls[5];
    for (int i=0; i<5; i++)
    {
        white_balls[i] = atoi(argv[2+i]);
    }

    int result = calculate_result(white_balls, power_ball);

    printf("%d percent chance of winning\n", result);

    return 0;
}
```

Typical of most initial implementations, this is missing a lot of features. But it's a good place to begin. Before committing his code, he wants to make sure it compiles and runs.

```
lottery harry$ gcc -std=c99 lottery.c

lottery harry$ ls -l
total 32
-rwxr-xr-x  1 harry  staff  8904 May 17 07:56 a.out
-rw-r--r--  1 harry  staff   555 May 17 07:56 lottery.c
```

```
lottery harry$ ./a.out
Usage: ./a.out power_ball (5 white balls)

lottery harry$ ./a.out 42 1 2 3 4 5
0 percent chance of winning
```

Righto. Time to store this file in the repository. First Harry needs to add the file to the pending changeset.

```
lottery harry$ hg add lottery.c
```

Harry uses the status operation to make sure the pending changeset looks proper.

```
lottery harry$ hg status
A lottery.c
? a.out
```

Mercurial is complaining because it doesn't know what to do about that a.out file. Stiff upper lip and all that. That's a compiled executable, which should not be stored in a version control repository. He can just ignore that.[2] Now it's time to commit the file.

```
lottery harry$ hg commit -m "initial implementation"
```

3. Push, Pull, Log, Diff

Since this is Sally's first time using Mercurial on her desktop machine, she first sets up her .hgrc file.

```
[ui]
username = Sally <sally@futilisoft.com>
```

Now Sally needs to set up her own repository instance.

```
~ sally$ hg clone http://server.futilisoft.com:8000/ ./lottery
no changes found
updating to branch default
0 files updated, 0 files merged, 0 files removed, 0 files unresolved

~ sally$ cd lottery

lottery sally$ ls -al
```

---

[2]Or he could add a.out to his .hgignore file.

```
total 0
drwxr-xr-x   3 sally  staff  102 May 17 08:00 .
drwxr-xr-x  19 sally  staff  646 May 17 08:00 ..
drwxr-xr-x   8 sally  staff  272 May 17 08:00 .hg
```

Hmmm. Harry was supposed to commit the initial code, but there's nothing here.

But Harry did commit his changes! Why aren't they here? Ah, he forgot to push. Sally screams at Harry loudly enough to be heard six time zones away.

```
lottery harry$ hg push
pushing to http://server.futilisoft.com:8000/
searching for changes
remote: adding changesets
remote: adding manifests
remote: adding file changes
remote: added 1 changesets with 1 changes to 1 files
```

Now Sally can pull.

```
lottery sally$ hg pull
pulling from http://server.futilisoft.com:8000/
requesting all changes
adding changesets
adding manifests
adding file changes
added 1 changesets with 1 changes to 1 files
(run 'hg update' to get a working copy)
```

> *The developers of Mercurial have done a great job on ease of use, including little prompts like the one I highlighted above. Mercurial is the friendliest DVCS around.*

Now that she has pulled, Sally should have the code, right?

```
lottery sally$ ls -al
total 0
drwxr-xr-x   3 sally  staff  102 May 17 08:00 .
drwxr-xr-x  20 sally  staff  680 May 17 08:06 ..
drwxr-xr-x  12 sally  staff  408 May 17 08:06 .hg
```

Hmmm. Still not there. Ah, maybe she needs to **hg update** the working copy.

```
lottery sally$ hg update
1 files updated, 0 files merged, 0 files removed, 0 files unresolved

lottery sally$ ls -al
total 8
drwxr-xr-x   4 sally   staff  136 May 17 08:07 .
drwxr-xr-x  20 sally   staff  680 May 17 08:06 ..
drwxr-xr-x  12 sally   staff  408 May 17 08:07 .hg
-rw-r--r--   1 sally   staff  555 May 17 08:07 lottery.c
```

Now that she has the initial code they had previously discussed, Sally is happy as a dead pig in the sunshine. She wants to check the log to see the details.

```
lottery sally$ hg log
changeset:   0:1f8baa59f5a4
tag:         tip
user:        Harry <harry@futilisoft.com>
date:        Tue May 17 07:58:36 2011 -0500
summary:     initial implementation
```

> *Note the way Mercurial describes this commit: 0:1f8baa59f5a4. At the lowest level, a Mercurial version ID is a SHA-1 hash, usually displayed in hex with only its first 12 characters. This is the part after the colon. Before the colon is a friendlier version number, one which starts at zero and increases by one with each new version. This is more intuitive, but these version numbers are valid only in one repository instance.*

When Sally decides to take a look at the code, she immediately finds something that makes her nervous as a chicken on a conveyor belt. The program expects the red ball number to be the first argument, followed by the other five. But in the actual lottery, the five white numbers are always drawn and shown first. She worries this will be confusing for users so she decides to fix it. Fortunately it is only necessary to modify a few lines of main().

```
    if (argc != 7)
    {
        fprintf(stderr, "Usage: %s (5 white balls) power_ball\n", argv[0]);
        return -1;
    }

    int power_ball = atoi(argv[6]);

    int white_balls[5];
    for (int i=0; i<5; i++)
    {
        white_balls[i] = atoi(argv[1+i]);
    }
```

Now she uses the **status** operation to see the pending changes.

```
lottery sally$ hg status
M lottery.c
```

No surprise there. Mercurial knows that `lottery.c` has been modified. She wants to double-check by reviewing the actual changes.

```
lottery sally$ hg diff
diff -r 1f8baa59f5a4 lottery.c
--- a/lottery.c Tue May 17 07:58:36 2011 -0500
+++ b/lottery.c Tue May 17 08:09:58 2011 -0500
@@ -11,16 +11,16 @@
 {
     if (argc != 7)
     {
-        fprintf(stderr, "Usage: %s power_ball (5 white balls)\n", argv[0]);
+        fprintf(stderr, "Usage: %s (5 white balls) power_ball\n", argv[0]);
         return -1;
     }

-    int power_ball = atoi(argv[1]);
+    int power_ball = atoi(argv[6]);

     int white_balls[5];
     for (int i=0; i<5; i++)
     {
-        white_balls[i] = atoi(argv[2+i]);
+        white_balls[i] = atoi(argv[1+i]);
     }

     int result = calculate_result(white_balls, power_ball);
```

Ain't that the bee's knees!?!

4. Update, Commit (with a merge)

Meanwhile, Harry has been coding as well. He heard somebody say that it's best to compile with all the warnings turned on, so he decides to give it a try.

```
lottery harry$ gcc -std=c99 -Wall -Wextra -Werror lottery.c
cc1: warnings being treated as errors
lottery.c:5: warning: unused parameter 'white_balls'
lottery.c:5: warning: unused parameter 'power_ball'
```

I say! The code has some warnings. The calculate_result() function isn't using its parameters. Harry looks at the situation and realises the problem immediately: That function should be checking its arguments for validity! The power ball can be from 1 to 39 inclusive. The white balls can be 1 to 59 inclusive. So he implements the error checking.

```
int calculate_result(int white_balls[5], int power_ball)
{
    for (int i=0; i<5; i++)
    {
        if (
              (white_balls[i] < 1)
              || (white_balls[i] > 59)
            )
        {
            return -1;
        }
    }

    if (
          (power_ball < 1)
          || (power_ball > 39)
        )
    {
        return -1;
    }

    return 0;
}
```

Grand. Let's see if it compiles.

```
lottery harry$ gcc -std=c99 -Wall -Wextra -Werror lottery.c

lottery harry$ ls -l
total 32
-rwxr-xr-x  1 harry  staff  8904 May 17 08:17 a.out
-rw-r--r--  1 harry  staff   843 May 17 08:16 lottery.c
```

Quite. But Harry decides to diff before committing, just for good measure.

```
lottery harry$ hg diff
diff -r 1f8baa59f5a4 lottery.c
--- a/lottery.c Tue May 17 07:58:36 2011 -0500
+++ b/lottery.c Tue May 17 08:17:53 2011 -0500
@@ -4,6 +4,25 @@

 int calculate_result(int white_balls[5], int power_ball)
 {
+    for (int i=0; i<5; i++)
+    {
+        if (
+            (white_balls[i] < 1)
+            || (white_balls[i] > 59)
+        )
+        {
+            return -1;
+        }
+    }
+
+    if (
+        (power_ball < 1)
+        || (power_ball > 39)
+    )
+    {
+        return -1;
+    }
+
     return 0;
 }
```

Good show. Time to commit the change.

```
lottery harry$ hg commit -m "fix some warnings"
```

No problems there. This time he remembers that he needs to push his changes to the server.

But Sally has been working at the same time and she had her change ready to commit and push first.

```
lottery sally$ hg commit -m "change order of the command line args to be \
                             more like what the user will expect"

lottery sally$ hg push
pushing to http://server.futilisoft.com:8000/
searching for changes
```

```
remote: adding changesets
remote: adding manifests
remote: adding file changes
remote: added 1 changesets with 1 changes to 1 files
```

So Harry tries to push his changes.

```
lottery harry$ hg push
pushing to http://server.futilisoft.com:8000/
searching for changes
abort: push creates new remote heads on branch 'default'!
(you should pull and merge or use push -f to force)
```

What's all this then? Mercurial is not allowing Harry to push his change because it would result in the default branch having two heads.

> *This restriction is analogous to the way the second generation tools refuse to allow a commit if it was not based on the most recent version in the repository. Mercurial allows this behavior to be overridden, but for most situations it is friendlier to the other members of the team if you do the pull and merge before you push.*

Harry uses pull to bring in changes.

```
lottery harry$ hg pull
pulling from http://server.futilisoft.com:8000/
searching for changes
adding changesets
adding manifests
adding file changes
added 1 changesets with 1 changes to 1 files (+1 heads)
(run 'hg heads' to see heads, 'hg merge' to merge)
```

Following the instructions from Mercurial's output, Harry wants to see what **hg heads** has to say.

```
lottery harry$ hg heads
changeset:   2:7dd1d2434f80
tag:         tip
parent:      0:1f8baa59f5a4
```

```
user:       Sally <sally@futilisoft.com>
date:       Tue May 17 08:25:22 2011 -0500
summary:    change order of the command line args to be \
            more like what the user will expect

changeset:  1:efcd0b05ec2c
user:       Harry <harry@futilisoft.com>
date:       Tue May 17 08:24:01 2011 -0500
summary:    fix some warnings
```

Harry wonders why he can't just update.

```
lottery harry$ hg update
abort: crosses branches (merge branches or use --check to force update)
```

That didn't work. OK, maybe a merge.

```
lottery harry$ hg merge
merging lottery.c
0 files updated, 1 files merged, 0 files removed, 0 files unresolved
(branch merge, don't forget to commit)
```

Great! Now the merge is in the working copy.

```
lottery harry$ hg status
M lottery.c
? a.out
```

Everything seems to be proper good. Harry wants to see what happened.

```
lottery harry$ hg diff
diff -r efcd0b05ec2c lottery.c
--- a/lottery.c Tue May 17 08:24:01 2011 -0500
+++ b/lottery.c Tue May 17 08:30:00 2011 -0500
@@ -30,16 +30,16 @@
 {
     if (argc != 7)
     {
-        fprintf(stderr, "Usage: %s power_ball (5 white balls)\n", argv[0]);
+        fprintf(stderr, "Usage: %s (5 white balls) power_ball\n", argv[0]);
         return -1;
     }

-    int power_ball = atoi(argv[1]);
+    int power_ball = atoi(argv[6]);

     int white_balls[5];
     for (int i=0; i<5; i++)
     {
-        white_balls[i] = atoi(argv[2+i]);
```

```
+            white_balls[i] = atoi(argv[1+i]);
      }

      int result = calculate_result(white_balls, power_ball);
```

Interesting. Diff shows Sally's changes. This is because the diff was performed against changeset efcd0b05ec2c. Harry types **hg parents** to see the version of the tree on which his current pending changeset is based.

```
lottery harry$ hg parents
changeset:   1:efcd0b05ec2c
user:        Harry <harry@futilisoft.com>
date:        Tue May 17 08:24:01 2011 -0500
summary:     fix some warnings

changeset:   2:7dd1d2434f80
tag:         tip
parent:      0:1f8baa59f5a4
user:        Sally <sally@futilisoft.com>
date:        Tue May 17 08:25:22 2011 -0500
summary:     change order of the command line args to be \
             more like what the user will expect
```

Because it is a merge in progress, his working copy has **two** parents. The resulting DAG node will have two parents as well.

His code is already committed. Apparently Mercurial was able to merge Sally's changes directly into Harry's modified copy of the file without any conflicts. Smashing! Let's see if it compiles.

```
lottery harry$ gcc -std=c99 -Wall -Wextra -Werror lottery.c

lottery harry$ ls -l
total 32
-rwxr-xr-x  1 harry  staff  8904 May 17 08:34 a.out
-rw-r--r--  1 harry  staff   843 May 17 08:28 lottery.c
```

Very well then. So Harry is ready to commit the merge.

```
lottery harry$ hg commit -m "merge"
```

And now **hg parents** shows only one node but that node has two parents.

```
lottery harry$ hg parents
changeset:   3:edbf336fe3fa
tag:         tip
parent:      1:efcd0b05ec2c
```

```
parent:      2:7dd1d2434f80
user:        Harry <harry@futilisoft.com>
date:        Tue May 17 08:35:28 2011 -0500
summary:     merge
```

And push.

```
lottery harry$ hg push
pushing to http://server.futilisoft.com:8000/
searching for changes
remote: adding changesets
remote: adding manifests
remote: adding file changes
remote: added 2 changesets with 2 changes to 1 files
```

5. Update (with merge)

Meanwhile, Sally is fixin' to go ahead and add a feature that was requested by the sales team: If the user chooses the lucky number 7 as the red ball, the chances of winning are doubled. Since she is starting a new task, she decides to begin with a pull and update to make sure she has the latest code.

```
lottery sally$ hg pull
pulling from http://server.futilisoft.com:8000/
searching for changes
adding changesets
adding manifests
adding file changes
added 2 changesets with 2 changes to 1 files
(run 'hg update' to get a working copy)

lottery sally$ hg update
1 files updated, 0 files merged, 0 files removed, 0 files unresolved

lottery sally$ hg parents
changeset:   3:edbf336fe3fa
tag:         tip
parent:      2:efcd0b05ec2c
parent:      1:7dd1d2434f80
user:        Harry <harry@futilisoft.com>
date:        Tue May 17 08:35:28 2011 -0500
summary:     merge
```

Then she implements the lucky 7 feature in two shakes of a lamb's tail by adding just a few lines of new code to main().

```
lottery sally$ hg diff
diff -r edbf336fe3fa lottery.c
--- a/lottery.c Tue May 17 08:35:28 2011 -0500
+++ b/lottery.c Tue May 17 08:45:34 2011 -0500
@@ -44,6 +44,11 @@

    int result = calculate_result(white_balls, power_ball);

+    if (7 == power_ball)
+    {
+        result = result * 2;
+    }
+
    printf("%d percent chance of winning\n", result);

    return 0;
```

And commits her change. And pushes it too.

```
lottery sally$ hg commit -m "lucky 7"

lottery sally$ hg push
pushing to http://server.futilisoft.com:8000/
searching for changes
remote: adding changesets
remote: adding manifests
remote: adding file changes
remote: added 1 changesets with 1 changes to 1 files
```

Meanwhile, Harry has realised his last change had a bug. He modified `calcu-late_result()` to return -1 for invalid arguments but he forgot to modify the caller to handle the error. As a consequence, entering a ball number that is out of range causes the program to behave improperly.

```
lottery harry$ ./a.out 61 2 3 4 5 42
-1 percent chance of winning
```

The percent chance of winning certainly can't be a negative number, now can it? So Harry adds an extra check for this case.

```
lottery harry$ hg diff
diff -r edbf336fe3fa lottery.c
--- a/lottery.c Tue May 17 08:35:28 2011 -0500
+++ b/lottery.c Tue May 17 10:15:19 2011 -0500
@@ -44,6 +44,12 @@

    int result = calculate_result(white_balls, power_ball);

+    if (result < 0)
```

```
+   {
+       fprintf(stderr, "Invalid arguments\n");
+       return -1;
+   }
+

    printf("%d percent chance of winning\n", result);

    return 0;
```

And proceeds to commit and push the fix.

```
lottery harry$ hg commit -m "propagate error code"

lottery harry$ hg push
pushing to http://server.futilisoft.com:8000/
searching for changes
abort: push creates new remote heads on branch 'default'!
(you should pull and merge or use push -f to force)
```

Blimey! Sally must have pushed a new changeset already. Harry once again needs to pull and merge to combine Sally's changes with his own.

```
lottery harry$ hg pull
pulling from http://server.futilisoft.com:8000/
searching for changes
adding changesets
adding manifests
adding file changes
added 1 changesets with 1 changes to 1 files (+1 heads)
(run 'hg heads' to see heads, 'hg merge' to merge)
```

```
lottery harry$ hg merge
merging lottery.c
warning: conflicts during merge.
merging lottery.c failed!
0 files updated, 0 files merged, 0 files removed, 1 files unresolved
use 'hg resolve' to retry unresolved file merges or 'hg update -C .' to abandon
```

The merge didn't go quite as smoothly this time. Harry wonders if anyone would notice if he were to leg it down to the pub. Apparently there was a conflict. Harry decides to open up lottery.c in his editor to examine the situation.

```
...
    int result = calculate_result(white_balls, power_ball);

<<<<<<< local
    if (result < 0)
=======
    if (7 == power_ball)
```

```
>>>>>>> other
    {
<<<<<<< local
        fprintf(stderr, "Invalid arguments\n");
        return -1;
=======
        result = result * 2;
>>>>>>> other
    }

    printf("%d percent chance of winning\n", result);

    return 0;
...
```

Mercurial has included both Harry's code and Sally's code with conflict markers to delimit things. What we want is to include both blocks of code. Sally's new code can simply be included right after Harry's error checking.

```
...
    int result = calculate_result(white_balls, power_ball);

    if (result < 0)
    {
        fprintf(stderr, "Invalid arguments\n");
        return -1;
    }

    if (7 == power_ball)
    {
        result = result * 2;
    }

    printf("%d percent chance of winning\n", result);

    return 0;
...
```

That should take care of the problem. Harry compiles the code to make sure and commits the merge.

```
lottery harry$ hg commit -m "merge"
abort: unresolved merge conflicts (see hg resolve)
```

Crikey! Now what? Harry fixed the conflict in lottery.c but Mercurial doesn't seem to know that. The output suggested **hg resolve**.

```
lottery harry$ hg resolve -l
U lottery.c
```

Ah yes. Harry realises that he forgot to tell Mercurial that he had resolved the conflict. He uses **resolve** to let Mercurial know that the problem has been dealt with.

```
lottery harry$ hg resolve -m lottery.c

lottery harry$ hg resolve -l
R lottery.c
```

There, that looks much better. Harry tries again to commit the merge.

```
lottery harry$ hg commit -m "merge"
```

And then to retry the push.

```
lottery harry$ hg push
pushing to http://server.futilisoft.com:8000/
searching for changes
remote: adding changesets
remote: adding manifests
remote: adding file changes
remote: added 2 changesets with 2 changes to 1 files
```

And... that's the last wicket.

6. Move

Harry immediately moves on to his next task, which is to restructure the tree a bit. He doesn't want the top level of the repository to get too cluttered so he decides to move their vast number of source code files into a src subdirectory.

```
lottery harry$ mkdir src

lottery harry$ hg move lottery.c src

lottery harry$ hg st
A src/lottery.c
R lottery.c
? a.out

lottery harry$ hg commit -m "dir structure"

lottery harry$ hg push
pushing to http://server.futilisoft.com:8000/
searching for changes
```

```
remote: adding changesets
remote: adding manifests
remote: adding file changes
remote: added 1 changesets with 1 changes to 1 files
```

Sally decides having the number 7 as a constant in the code is ugly enough to scare a bulldog off a meat truck. She adds a #define to give it a more meaningful name.

```
lottery sally$ hg diff
diff -r 4031ca2d74bf lottery.c
--- a/lottery.c Tue May 17 11:01:04 2011 -0500
+++ b/lottery.c Tue May 17 11:30:14 2011 -0500
@@ -2,6 +2,8 @@
 #include <stdio.h>
 #include <stdlib.h>

+#define LUCKY_NUMBER 7
+
 int calculate_result(int white_balls[5], int power_ball)
 {
     for (int i=0; i<5; i++)
@@ -50,7 +52,7 @@
         return -1;
     }

-    if (7 == power_ball)
+    if (LUCKY_NUMBER == power_ball)
     {
         result = result * 2;
     }
```

And immediately commits and pushes the change.

```
lottery sally$ hg commit -m "use a #define for the lucky number"

lottery sally$ hg push
pushing to http://server.futilisoft.com:8000/
searching for changes
abort: push creates new remote heads on branch 'default'!
(you should pull and merge or use push -f to force)
```

Hmmm. Sally needs to pull and merge before she can push her changes.

```
lottery sally$ hg pull
pulling from http://server.futilisoft.com:8000/
searching for changes
adding changesets
adding manifests
adding file changes
added 1 changesets with 1 changes to 1 files (+1 heads)
(run 'hg heads' to see heads, 'hg merge' to merge)
```

She uses **hg heads** to see about the merge that needs to be done.

```
lottery sally$ hg heads
changeset:   8:b9ea7a983ae6
tag:         tip
parent:      6:4031ca2d74bf
user:        Harry <harry@futilisoft.com>
date:        Tue May 17 11:24:58 2011 -0500
summary:     dir structure

changeset:   7:7492d7fa4427
user:        Sally <sally@futilisoft.com>
date:        Tue May 17 11:31:26 2011 -0500
summary:     use a #define for the lucky number
```

The **hg merge** command performs the merge work and leaves the result in her working copy, waiting to be committed.

```
lottery sally$ hg merge
merging lottery.c and src/lottery.c to src/lottery.c
0 files updated, 1 files merged, 0 files removed, 0 files unresolved
(branch merge, don't forget to commit)

lottery sally$ hg st
M src/lottery.c
R lottery.c
? a.out
```

And she commits the merge and pushes it up to the server.

```
lottery sally$ hg commit -m "merge"

lottery sally$ hg push
pushing to http://server.futilisoft.com:8000/
searching for changes
remote: adding changesets
remote: adding manifests
remote: adding file changes
remote: added 2 changesets with 2 changes to 2 files
```

7. Rename

Harry decides the time has come to create a proper Makefile. And also to gratuitously rename lottery.c.

```
lottery harry$ hg add Makefile

lottery harry$ hg rename src/lottery.c src/pb.c

lottery harry$ hg st
A Makefile
A src/pb.c
R src/lottery.c

lottery harry$ hg commit -m "Makefile. and lottery.c was too long to type."

lottery harry$ hg push
pushing to http://server.futilisoft.com:8000/
searching for changes
remote: adding changesets
remote: adding manifests
remote: adding file changes
remote: added 1 changesets with 2 changes to 2 files
```

Sally maintains her momentum with #define and adds names for the ball ranges.

```
lottery sally$ hg diff
diff -r c3e40a7996f0 src/lottery.c
--- a/src/lottery.c Tue May 17 11:36:12 2011 -0500
+++ b/src/lottery.c Tue May 17 11:50:23 2011 -0500
@@ -3,6 +3,8 @@
 #include <stdlib.h>

 #define LUCKY_NUMBER 7
+#define MAX_WHITE_BALL 59
+#define MAX_POWER_BALL 39

 int calculate_result(int white_balls[5], int power_ball)
 {
@@ -10,7 +12,7 @@
     {
         if (
             (white_balls[i] < 1)
-            || (white_balls[i] > 59)
+            || (white_balls[i] > MAX_WHITE_BALL)
         )
         {
             return -1;
@@ -19,7 +21,7 @@

     if (
         (power_ball < 1)
-        || (power_ball > 39)
+        || (power_ball > MAX_POWER_BALL)
     )
     {
         return -1;
```

And commits her changes.

```
lottery sally$ hg commit -m "more #defines"

lottery sally$ hg push
pushing to http://server.futilisoft.com:8000/
searching for changes
abort: push creates new remote heads on branch 'default'!
(you should pull and merge or use push -f to force)
```

Grrr. That Harry is dumber than a sack full of hammers.

```
lottery sally$ hg pull
pulling from http://server.futilisoft.com:8000/
searching for changes
adding changesets
adding manifests
adding file changes
added 1 changesets with 2 changes to 2 files (+1 heads)
(run 'hg heads' to see heads, 'hg merge' to merge)

lottery sally$ hg heads
changeset:    11:346dd1ab5474
tag:          tip
parent:       9:c3e40a7996f0
user:         Harry <harry@futilisoft.com>
date:         Tue May 17 11:48:57 2011 -0500
summary:      Makefile. and lottery.c was too long to type.

changeset:    10:51a8540dbb7e
user:         Sally <sally@futilisoft.com>
date:         Tue May 17 11:51:24 2011 -0500
summary:      more #defines

lottery sally$ hg merge
merging src/lottery.c and src/pb.c to src/pb.c
1 files updated, 1 files merged, 0 files removed, 0 files unresolved
(branch merge, don't forget to commit)
```

Note that Mercurial correctly handled this merge, even though the same file had been modified in one branch and renamed in the other.

```
lottery sally$ cd ..

lottery sally$ make
gcc -std=c99 -Wall -Wextra -Werror src/pb.c -o pb

lottery sally$ hg commit -m "merge"

lottery sally$ hg push
pushing to http://server.futilisoft.com:8000/
searching for changes
remote: adding changesets
remote: adding manifests
remote: adding file changes
remote: added 2 changesets with 2 changes to 2 files
```

8. Delete

Harry wants to get a head start on Zawinski's Law, so he decides to add an IMAP protocol library to their tree.

```
lottery harry$ hg add libvmime-0.9.1
adding libvmime-0.9.1/AUTHORS
adding libvmime-0.9.1/COPYING
adding libvmime-0.9.1/ChangeLog
adding libvmime-0.9.1/HACKING
adding libvmime-0.9.1/INSTALL
adding libvmime-0.9.1/Makefile.am
...

lottery harry$ hg commit -m "add libvmime so we can do the mail reader feature"

lottery harry$ hg push
pushing to http://server.futilisoft.com:8000/
searching for changes
remote: adding changesets
remote: adding manifests
remote: adding file changes
remote: added 1 changesets with 387 changes to 387 files
```

Sally does a pull and finds something that makes her want to jerk Harry through a knot.

```
lottery sally$ hg pull
pulling from http://server.futilisoft.com:8000/
searching for changes
adding changesets
adding manifests
adding file changes
added 1 changesets with 387 changes to 387 files
```

```
(run 'hg update' to get a working copy)

lottery sally$ hg update
387 files updated, 0 files merged, 0 files removed, 0 files unresolved
```

Sally remembers that the specification says the product isn't supposed to include a full email reader until the next release. For the entire 1.0 development cycle, that third party library is going to be about as useful as a screen door on a submarine. So she deletes it.

```
lottery sally$ hg remove libvmime-0.9.1
removing libvmime-0.9.1/AUTHORS
removing libvmime-0.9.1/COPYING
removing libvmime-0.9.1/ChangeLog
removing libvmime-0.9.1/HACKING
removing libvmime-0.9.1/INSTALL
removing libvmime-0.9.1/Makefile.am
...

lottery sally$ hg commit -m "no mail reader until 2.0"

lottery sally$ hg push
pushing to http://server.futilisoft.com:8000/
searching for changes
remote: adding changesets
remote: adding manifests
remote: adding file changes
remote: added 1 changesets with 0 changes to 0 files
```

9. Revert

In the Subversion example, this is the place where Sally asks for a lock. But Mercurial doesn't support lock.

Harry updates his repository instance.

```
lottery harry$ hg pull
pulling from http://server.futilisoft.com:8000/
searching for changes
adding changesets
adding manifests
adding file changes
```

```
added 1 changesets with 0 changes to 0 files
(run 'hg update' to get a working copy)

lottery harry$ hg update
0 files updated, 0 files merged, 387 files removed, 0 files unresolved

lottery harry$ ls -l
total 8
-rw-r--r--  1 harry  staff   66 May 17 11:47 Makefile
drwxr-xr-x  3 harry  staff  102 May 17 13:58 src
```

Sod it! That Sally must have her landlady face on. She's deleted all his email code! Harry decides to indent[3] pb.c.

```
lottery harry$ indent src/pb.c

lottery harry$ hg st
M src/pb.c
? pb.c.BAK
```

This is getting shambolic. Harry calms down and reverts the changes.

```
lottery harry$ hg revert src/pb.c

lottery harry$ hg st
? pb.c.BAK
? src/pb.c.orig

lottery harry$ rm pb.c.BAK src/pb.c.orig
```

Sally has decided to eliminate uses of atoi(), which is deprecated.

```
lottery sally$ hg diff
diff -r a3a4497e7ff6 src/pb.c
--- a/src/pb.c  Tue May 17 14:04:44 2011 -0500
+++ b/src/pb.c  Tue May 17 14:10:51 2011 -0500
@@ -43,7 +43,14 @@
     int white_balls[5];
     for (int i=0; i<5; i++)
     {
-        white_balls[i] = atoi(argv[1+i]);
+        char* endptr = NULL;
+        long val = strtol(argv[1+i], &endptr, 10);
+        if (*endptr)
+        {
+            fprintf(stderr, "Invalid arguments\n");
+            return -1;
+        }
```

---

[3]http://en.wikipedia.org/wiki/Indent_(Unix)

```
+        white_balls[i] = (int) val;
    }

    int result = calculate_result(white_balls, power_ball);

lottery sally$ make
gcc -std=c99 -Wall -Wextra -Werror pb.c -o pb

lottery sally$ ./pb 1 2 3 4 5 6
0 percent chance of winning

lottery sally$ ./pb 1 2 3e 4 5 6
Invalid arguments
```

And she commits her changes, easy as dialing BR-549.

```
lottery sally$ hg commit -m "use strtol. atoi is deprecated."

lottery sally$ hg push
pushing to http://server.futilisoft.com:8000/
searching for changes
remote: adding changesets
remote: adding manifests
remote: adding file changes
remote: added 1 changesets with 1 changes to 1 files
```

10. Tag

Grieving the loss of his email code, Harry creates a tag so he can quickly find it.

```
lottery harry$ hg log
...
changeset:   13:4ac7113cd126
user:        Harry <harry@futilisoft.com>
date:        Tue May 17 14:01:51 2011 -0500
summary:     add libvmime so we can do the mail reader feature
...

lottery harry$ hg tag -r 4ac7113cd126 just_before_sally_deleted_my_email_code
```

Harry could have typed -r 13, using the local revision number instead of the changeset ID.

```
lottery harry$ hg log
changeset:   16:f282002d72ee
tag:         tip
user:        Harry <harry@futilisoft.com>
date:        Tue May 17 14:14:44 2011 -0500
summary:     Added tag just_before_sally_deleted_my_email_code for changeset 4ac7113cd126

changeset:   15:8ac66a135f35
user:        Sally <sally@futilisoft.com>
date:        Tue May 17 14:11:45 2011 -0500
summary:     use strtol. atoi is deprecated.

changeset:   14:a3a4497e7ff6
user:        Sally <sally@futilisoft.com>
date:        Tue May 17 14:04:44 2011 -0500
summary:     no mail reader until 2.0

changeset:   13:4ac7113cd126
tag:         just_before_sally_deleted_my_email_code
user:        Harry <harry@futilisoft.com>
date:        Tue May 17 14:01:51 2011 -0500
summary:     add libvmime so we can do the mail reader feature
...
```

I gotta admit I'm not too fond of the way Mercurial handles tags. They're stored in a special .hgtags file in the version control tree. This means that applying a tag causes another commit. If you want your continuous integration system to apply a tag to mark the revision on which every build is done, you have to teach it to ignore changesets where nothing happened except the addition of a tag; otherwise it'll tag itself into an infinite loop.

```
lottery harry$ hg push
pushing to http://server.futilisoft.com:8000/
searching for changes
remote: adding changesets
remote: adding manifests
remote: adding file changes
remote: added 1 changesets with 1 changes to 1 files
```

Sally sees Harry gloating in the company chat room about his beloved tag, so she does an update.

```
lottery sally$ hg pull
pulling from http://server.futilisoft.com:8000/
searching for changes
adding changesets
adding manifests
adding file changes
added 1 changesets with 1 changes to 1 files
(run 'hg update' to get a working copy)

lottery sally$ hg update
1 files updated, 0 files merged, 0 files removed, 0 files unresolved

lottery sally$ hg parents
changeset:   16:f282002d72ee
tag:         tip
user:        Harry <harry@futilisoft.com>
date:        Tue May 17 14:14:44 2011 -0500
summary:     Added tag just_before_sally_deleted_my_email_code for changeset 4ac7113cd126
```

Sally sees Harry's tag and rolls her eyes. Fine. Whatever.

11. Branch

Sally wants more privacy. She decides to create her own named branch.

```
lottery sally$ hg branch no_boys_allowed
marked working directory as branch no_boys_allowed
```

In its very early days, Mercurial was designed to support branching by having one repository instance per branch. This approach turned out to not be flexible enough, so the developers added named branches, a way of associating a name with a line of development. This approach allows multiple branches to exist within a single repository instance.

Now that Sally is working in her own branch, she feels much more productive. She adds support for the "favorite" option. When a user is playing her favorite numbers, her chances of winning should be doubled. In doing this, she had to rework the way command-line args are parsed. And she removes an atoi() call she missed last time. And she restructures all the error checking into one place.

So main() now looks like this:

```c
int main(int argc, char** argv)
{
    int balls[6];
    int count_balls = 0;
    int favorite = 0;

    for (int i=1; i<argc; i++)
    {
        const char* arg = argv[i];

        if ('-' == arg[0])
        {
            if (0 == strcmp(arg, "-favorite"))
            {
                favorite = 1;
            }
            else
            {
                goto usage_error;
            }
        }
        else
        {
            char* endptr = NULL;
            long val = strtol(arg, &endptr, 10);
            if (*endptr)
            {
                goto usage_error;
            }
            balls[count_balls++] = (int) val;
        }
    }

    if (6 != count_balls)
    {
        goto usage_error;
    }

    int power_ball = balls[5];

    int result = calculate_result(balls, power_ball);

    if (result < 0)
    {
        goto usage_error;
```

```
    }

    if (LUCKY_NUMBER == power_ball)
    {
        result = result * 2;
    }

    if (favorite)
    {
        result = result * 2;
    }

    printf("%d percent chance of winning\n", result);

    return 0;

usage_error:
    fprintf(stderr, "Usage: %s [-favorite] (5 white balls) power_ball\n", argv[0]);
    return -1;
}
```

She commits her changes, knowing that the commit will succeed because she is working in her private branch.

```
lottery sally$ hg commit -m "add -favorite and cleanup some other stuff"

lottery sally$ hg push
pushing to http://server.futilisoft.com:8000/
searching for changes
abort: push creates new remote branches: no_boys_allowed!
(use 'hg push --new-branch' to create new remote branches)
```

Hey! What's the problem here? Ah, Mercurial just wants Sally to be more explicit about the fact that she's creating a new branch.

```
lottery sally$ hg push --new-branch
pushing to http://server.futilisoft.com:8000/
searching for changes
remote: adding changesets
remote: adding manifests
remote: adding file changes
remote: added 1 changesets with 1 changes to 1 files
```

12. Merge (no conflicts)

Meanwhile, over in the default branch, Harry decides the white balls should be sorted before analysing them, because that's how they are on the box.

```
lottery harry$ hg diff
diff -r f282002d72ee src/pb.c
--- a/src/pb.c  Tue May 17 14:14:44 2011 -0500
+++ b/src/pb.c  Tue May 17 14:26:36 2011 -0500
@@ -6,6 +6,25 @@
 #define MAX_WHITE_BALL 59
 #define MAX_POWER_BALL 39

+static int my_sort_func(const void* p1, const void* p2)
+{
+    int v1 = *((int *) p1);
+    int v2 = *((int *) p2);
+
+    if (v1 < v2)
+    {
+        return -1;
+    }
+    else if (v1 > v2)
+    {
+        return 1;
+    }
+    else
+    {
+        return 0;
+    }
+}
+
 int calculate_result(int white_balls[5], int power_ball)
 {
     for (int i=0; i<5; i++)
@@ -27,6 +46,8 @@
         return -1;
     }

+    qsort(white_balls, 5, sizeof(int), my_sort_func);
+
     return 0;
 }
```

And he commits the change.

```
lottery harry$ hg commit -m "sort the white balls"
```

But now he's curious about what Sally has been doing. She said he wasn't allowed to commit to her branch but she didn't say anything about **looking** at it.

```
lottery harry$ hg log
changeset:   18:3e1b620bb7ad
tag:         tip
parent:      16:f282002d72ee
user:        Harry <harry@futilisoft.com>
date:        Tue May 17 14:27:37 2011 -0500
```

```
summary:     sort the white balls

changeset:   17:836e4df60a27
branch:      no_boys_allowed
user:        Sally <sally@futilisoft.com>
date:        Tue May 17 14:24:14 2011 -0500
summary:     add -favorite and cleanup some other stuff
```

Interesting. She added the "favorite" feature. Harry decides he wants that. So he asks Mercurial to merge stuff from Sally's branch into the default branch.

```
lottery harry$ hg merge -r 836e4df60a27
merging src/pb.c
0 files updated, 1 files merged, 0 files removed, 0 files unresolved
(branch merge, don't forget to commit)
```

Brilliant! Harry examines pb.c and discovers that it was merged correctly. Sally's "favorite" changes are there and his qsort changes are as well. So he compiles the code, runs a quick test, and commits the merge.

```
lottery harry$ make
gcc -std=c99 -Wall -Wextra -Werror pb.c -o pb

lottery harry$ ./pb -favorite 5 3 33 22 7 31
0 percent chance of winning

lottery harry$ hg commit -m "merge changes from sally"

lottery harry$ hg push
pushing to http://server.futilisoft.com:8000/
searching for changes
remote: adding changesets
remote: adding manifests
remote: adding file changes
remote: added 2 changesets with 2 changes to 1 files
```

13. Merge (repeated, no conflicts)

Simultaneously, both Harry and Sally have a crisis of conscience and realize that their code has no comments at all.

Harry:

```
lottery harry$ hg diff
diff -r 922ff5acda79 src/pb.c
--- a/src/pb.c  Tue May 17 14:31:41 2011 -0500
+++ b/src/pb.c  Tue May 17 14:39:21 2011 -0500
```

```
@@ -47,6 +47,7 @@
        return -1;
    }

+    // lottery ball numbers are always shown sorted
    qsort(white_balls, 5, sizeof(int), my_sort_func);

    return 0;

lottery harry$ hg commit -m comments

lottery harry$ hg push
pushing to http://server.futilisoft.com:8000/
searching for changes
remote: adding changesets
remote: adding manifests
remote: adding file changes
remote: added 1 changesets with 1 changes to 1 files
```

And Sally:

```
lottery sally$ hg diff
diff -r 836e4df60a27 src/pb.c
--- a/src/pb.c  Tue May 17 14:24:14 2011 -0500
+++ b/src/pb.c  Tue May 17 14:40:27 2011 -0500
@@ -35,7 +35,7 @@
 {
     int balls[6];
     int count_balls = 0;
-    int favorite = 0;
+    int favorite = 0;  // this should be a bool

     for (int i=1; i<argc; i++)
     {
@@ -69,10 +69,13 @@
        goto usage_error;
    }

+    // the power ball is always the last one given
    int power_ball = balls[5];

    int result = calculate_result(balls, power_ball);

+    // calculate result can return -1 if the ball numbers
+    // are out of range
    if (result < 0)
    {
        goto usage_error;

lottery sally$ hg commit -m comments

lottery sally$ hg push
pushing to http://server.futilisoft.com:8000/
searching for changes
```

```
remote: adding changesets
remote: adding manifests
remote: adding file changes
remote: added 1 changesets with 1 changes to 1 files (+1 heads)
```

Harry decides to try again to merge the changes from Sally's branch.

```
lottery harry$ hg heads
changeset:   21:76fcfc4170dc
branch:      no_boys_allowed
tag:         tip
parent:      17:836e4df60a27
user:        Sally <sally@futilisoft.com>
date:        Tue May 17 14:44:56 2011 -0500
summary:     comments

changeset:   20:6ae39c9ee2e8
user:        Harry <harry@futilisoft.com>
date:        Tue May 17 14:45:04 2011 -0500
summary:     comments

lottery harry$ hg merge -r 21
merging src/pb.c
0 files updated, 1 files merged, 0 files removed, 0 files unresolved
(branch merge, don't forget to commit)
```

```
lottery harry$ hg diff
diff -r 6ae39c9ee2e8 src/pb.c
--- a/src/pb.c  Tue May 17 14:45:04 2011 -0500
+++ b/src/pb.c  Tue May 17 14:47:52 2011 -0500
@@ -57,7 +57,7 @@
 {
     int balls[6];
     int count_balls = 0;
-    int favorite = 0;
+    int favorite = 0;  // this should be a bool

     for (int i=1; i<argc; i++)
     {
@@ -91,10 +91,13 @@
         goto usage_error;
     }

+    // the power ball is always the last one given
     int power_ball = balls[5];

     int result = calculate_result(balls, power_ball);

+    // calculate result can return -1 if the ball numbers
```

```
+    // are out of range
     if (result < 0)
     {
         goto usage_error;
```

No worries on the merge then. Harry checks to see if everything compiles, and commits the merge.

```
lottery harry$ make
gcc -std=c99 -Wall -Wextra -Werror pb.c -o pb

lottery harry$ hg commit -m "merge changes from sally"

lottery harry$ hg push
pushing to http://server.futilisoft.com:8000/
searching for changes
remote: adding changesets
remote: adding manifests
remote: adding file changes
remote: added 1 changesets with 1 changes to 1 files (-1 heads)
```

14. Merge (conflicts)

Sally realizes that C99 has a bool type that should have been used.

```
lottery sally$ hg diff
diff -r 76fcfc4170dc src/pb.c
--- a/src/pb.c  Tue May 17 14:44:56 2011 -0500
+++ b/src/pb.c  Tue May 17 14:51:23 2011 -0500
@@ -2,6 +2,7 @@
 #include <stdio.h>
 #include <stdlib.h>
 #include <string.h>
+#include <stdbool.h>

 #define LUCKY_NUMBER 7
 #define MAX_WHITE_BALL 59
@@ -35,7 +36,7 @@
 {
     int balls[6];
     int count_balls = 0;
-    int favorite = 0;  // this should be a bool
+    bool favorite = false;

     for (int i=1; i<argc; i++)
     {
@@ -45,7 +46,7 @@
         {
             if (0 == strcmp(arg, "-favorite"))
             {
```

```
-            favorite = 1;
+            favorite = true;
        }
        else
        {
```

And she commits the change to her private branch.

```
lottery sally$ hg commit -m "use the bool type"

lottery sally$ hg push
pushing to http://server.futilisoft.com:8000/
searching for changes
remote: adding changesets
remote: adding manifests
remote: adding file changes
remote: added 1 changesets with 1 changes to 1 files (+1 heads)
```

Meanwhile, Harry has been grumbling about Sally's butchering of the Queen's English and decides to correct the spelling of the word "favourite".

```
lottery harry$ hg diff
diff -r e92fd20d2bc8 src/pb.c
--- a/src/pb.c  Tue May 17 14:49:12 2011 -0500
+++ b/src/pb.c  Tue May 17 14:53:11 2011 -0500
@@ -57,7 +57,7 @@
 {
     int balls[6];
     int count_balls = 0;
-    int favorite = 0;   // this should be a bool
+    int favourite = 0;   // this should be a bool

     for (int i=1; i<argc; i++)
     {
@@ -65,9 +65,9 @@

         if ('-' == arg[0])
         {
-            if (0 == strcmp(arg, "-favorite"))
+            if (0 == strcmp(arg, "-favourite"))
            {
-                favorite = 1;
+                favourite = 1;
            }
            else
            {
@@ -108,7 +108,7 @@
         result = result * 2;
     }

-    if (favorite)
+    if (favourite)
```

```
        {
            result = result * 2;
        }
@@ -118,7 +118,7 @@
        return 0;

    usage_error:
-       fprintf(stderr, "Usage: %s [-favorite] (5 white balls) power_ball\n", argv[0]);
+       fprintf(stderr, "Usage: %s [-favourite] (5 white balls) power_ball\n", argv[0]);
        return -1;
    }
```

Feeling quite chuffed about his pedantry, Harry proceeds to commit the change.

```
lottery harry$ hg commit -m "fixed spelling error"
```

And to once again merge Sally's changes into the default branch.

```
lottery harry$ hg merge -r 4f188690b962
merging src/pb.c
warning: conflicts during merge.
merging src/pb.c failed!
0 files updated, 0 files merged, 0 files removed, 1 files unresolved
use 'hg resolve' to retry unresolved file merges or 'hg update -C .' to abandon
```

Crikey! Conflicts in pb.c again.

```
lottery harry$ hg diff
diff -r a0c6fdbdd95f src/pb.c
--- a/src/pb.c  Tue May 17 14:53:41 2011 -0500
+++ b/src/pb.c  Tue May 17 14:55:08 2011 -0500
@@ -2,6 +2,7 @@
 #include <stdio.h>
 #include <stdlib.h>
 #include <string.h>
+#include <stdbool.h>

 #define LUCKY_NUMBER 7
 #define MAX_WHITE_BALL 59
@@ -57,7 +58,11 @@
 {
     int balls[6];
     int count_balls = 0;
+<<<<<<< .working
     int favourite = 0;  // this should be a bool
+=======
+    bool favorite = false;
+>>>>>>> .merge-right.r22

     for (int i=1; i<argc; i++)
     {
```

```
@@ -67,7 +72,11 @@
        {
            if (0 == strcmp(arg, "-favourite"))
            {
+<<<<<<< .working
                favourite = 1;
+=======
+                favorite = true;
+>>>>>>> .merge-right.r22
            }
            else
            {
```

That **is** a spot of bother. Harry quickly realises this conflict needs to be resolved manually by keeping the proper spelling but converting the type to bool like Sally did.

```
lottery harry$ hg diff
diff -r a0c6fdbdd95f src/pb.c
--- a/src/pb.c  Tue May 17 14:53:41 2011 -0500
+++ b/src/pb.c  Tue May 17 14:56:41 2011 -0500
@@ -2,6 +2,7 @@
 #include <stdio.h>
 #include <stdlib.h>
 #include <string.h>
+#include <stdbool.h>

 #define LUCKY_NUMBER 7
 #define MAX_WHITE_BALL 59
@@ -57,7 +58,7 @@
 {
     int balls[6];
     int count_balls = 0;
-    int favourite = 0;  // this should be a bool
+    bool favourite = false;

     for (int i=1; i<argc; i++)
     {
@@ -67,7 +68,7 @@
        {
            if (0 == strcmp(arg, "-favourite"))
            {
-                favourite = 1;
+                favourite = true;
            }
            else
            {
```

After manually merging the changes, Harry proceeds to resolve the conflict and commit the merge.

```
lottery harry$ hg resolve -m src/pb.c

lottery harry$ hg commit -m "merge, conflicts fixed"

lottery harry$ hg push
...
```

And all of Futilisoft's customers lived happily ever after.

15. Summary

The following table summarizes all 21 commands for Mercurial. See Table A.1 in Appendix A for a comparison of Mercurial's commands with other tools.

Operation	Mercurial Command
Create	hg init
Checkout	a
Commit	hg commit
Update	hg update
Add	hg add
Edit	b
Delete	hg remove
Rename	hg rename
Move	hg rename
Status	hg status
Diff	hg diff
Revert	hg revert
Log	hg log
Tag	hg tag^c
Branch	hg branch
Merge	hg merge
Resolve	hg resolve
Lock	d
Clone	hg clone
Push	hg push
Pull	hg pull

^aN/A: Mercurial keeps the repository instance inside the working copy.

[b]Automatic: Mercurial will notice that the file has changed.
[c]Tags are stored in a version-controlled text file. Causes a commit.
[d]Unsupported

8   Basics with Git

Futilisoft has begun work on a new product. This product calculates the probability (as an integer percentage) of winning the Powerball for any given set of numbers.

The company has assigned two developers to work on this new project, Harry, located in Birmingham, England, and Sally, located in Birmingham, Alabama. Both developers are telecommuting to the Futilisoft corporate headquarters in Cleveland. After a bit of discussion, they have decided to implement their product as a command-line app in C and to use Git[1] 1.7.5 for version control.

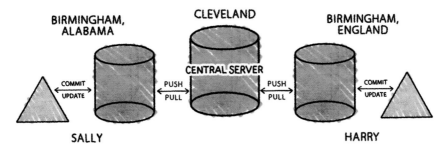

1. Create

Sally gets the project started by creating a new repository.

```
~ server$ mkdir lottery

~ server$ cd lottery

lottery server$ git init --bare lottery.git
```

---

[1]http://git-scm.com/

> *I consider the details of server configuration to be too much detail for this book. Just imagine that it happened. And that nothing went wrong.*

2. Clone, Add, Status, Commit

By this time Harry is done faffing about and is ready to start coding.

Since this is Harry's first time using Git, he first sets up his .gitconfig file with information that will be used to identify his commits in the log.

```
[user]
    name = Harry
    email = harry@futilisoft.com
```

Now he needs to get his own repository instance.

```
~ harry$ git clone http://server.futilisoft.com:8000/ ./lottery
Cloning into lottery...
warning: You appear to have cloned an empty repository.
```

> *Note that Git doesn't have a **checkout** command. Or rather, it has **git checkout**, but that command is equivalent to **Update**. Git keeps the repository instance within the administrative area of the working copy, so **git clone** actually performs both **clone** and **checkout**.*

Harry wonders if Sally has already done anything in the new repository.

```
~ harry$ ls -al lottery
total 0
drwxr-xr-x   3 harry  staff  102 May 17 07:55 .
drwxr-xr-x  21 harry  staff  714 May 17 07:55 ..
drwxr-xr-x   8 harry  staff  272 May 17 07:55 .git
```

Apparently not. Nothing here but the .git administrative area. Jolly good then. It's time to start coding. He opens his text editor and creates the starting point for their product.

```c
#include <stdio.h>
#include <stdlib.h>

int calculate_result(int white_balls[5], int power_ball)
{
    return 0;
}

int main(int argc, char** argv)
{
    if (argc != 7)
    {
        fprintf(stderr, "Usage: %s power_ball (5 white balls)\n", argv[0]);
        return -1;
    }

    int power_ball = atoi(argv[1]);

    int white_balls[5];
    for (int i=0; i<5; i++)
    {
        white_balls[i] = atoi(argv[2+i]);
    }

    int result = calculate_result(white_balls, power_ball);

    printf("%d percent chance of winning\n", result);

    return 0;
}
```

Typical of most initial implementations, this is missing a lot of features. But it's a good place to begin. Before committing his code, he wants to make sure it compiles and runs.

```
lottery harry$ gcc -std=c99 lottery.c

lottery harry$ ls -l
total 32
-rwxr-xr-x  1 harry  staff  8904 May 17 07:56 a.out
-rw-r--r--  1 harry  staff   555 May 17 07:56 lottery.c

lottery harry$ ./a.out
```

```
Usage: ./a.out power_ball (5 white balls)

lottery harry$ ./a.out 42 1 2 3 4 5
0 percent chance of winning
```

Righto. Time to store this file in the repository. First Harry needs to add the file to the Git staging area (which in Git's terminology is called the "index").

> *Note that Git's staging area is similar to my notion of the pending changeset, but the semantics are different. The pending changeset is a list of changes in the working copy. The Git staging area can contain things that are neither in the working copy nor the repository instance.*

```
lottery harry$ git add lottery.c
```

Harry uses the status operation to make sure the pending changeset looks proper.

```
lottery harry$ git status -s
A  lottery.c
?? a.out
```

Git is complaining because it doesn't know what to do about that a.out file. Don't panic! That's a compiled executable, which should not be stored in a version control repository. He can just ignore that. Now it's time to commit the file.

> *In my examples here I am showing **git commit** used with the -a flag. This makes **git commit** automatically detect modified files, like the other tools covered in this book. Without this flag, git wants you to explicitly **git add** any file which has been modified.*

```
lottery harry$ git commit -a -m "initial implementation"
[master (root-commit) 9a0ca10] initial implementation
 1 files changed, 30 insertions(+), 0 deletions(-)
 create mode 100644 lottery.c
```

3. Push, Pull, Log, Diff

Since this is Sally's first time using Git on her desktop machine, she first sets up her .gitconfig file.

```
[user]
    name = Sally
    email = sally@futilisoft.com
```

Now Sally needs to set up her own repository instance.

```
~ sally$ git clone http://server.futilisoft.com:8000/ ./lottery
Cloning into lottery...
warning: You appear to have cloned an empty repository.

~ sally$ cd lottery

lottery sally$ ls -al
total 0
drwxr-xr-x    3 sally  staff   102 May 17 08:00 .
drwxr-xr-x   19 sally  staff   646 May 17 08:00 ..
drwxr-xr-x    8 sally  staff   272 May 17 08:00 .git
```

Hmmm. Harry was supposed to commit the initial code, but there's nothing here.

But Harry did commit his changes! Why aren't they here? Ah, he forgot to push. Sally screams at Harry loudly enough to be heard across the Atlantic.

```
lottery harry$ git push
No refs in common and none specified; doing nothing.
Perhaps you should specify a branch such as 'master'.
fatal: The remote end hung up unexpectedly
error: failed to push some refs to 'http://server.futilisoft.com:8000/lottery'
```

By default, Git pushes only to matching branches: For every branch that exists on the local side, the remote side is updated if a branch of the same name already exists there. This means that you have to push the branch explicitly the first time.

```
lottery harry$ git push --all
Counting objects: 3, done.
Compressing objects: 100% (2/2), done.
Writing objects: 100% (3/3), 484 bytes, done.
Total 3 (delta 0), reused 0 (delta 0)
Unpacking objects: 100% (3/3), done.
To http://server.futilisoft.com:8000/lottery
 * [new branch]      master -> master
```

Now Sally can pull.

```
lottery sally$ git pull
remote: Counting objects: 3, done.
remote: Compressing objects: 100% (2/2), done.
remote: Total 3 (delta 0), reused 0 (delta 0)
Unpacking objects: 100% (3/3), done.
From http://server.futilisoft.com:8000/lottery
 * [new branch]      master      -> origin/master
```

Now that she has pulled, Sally has the code.

```
lottery sally$ ls -al
total 8
drwxr-xr-x   4 sally  staff  136 May 17 08:07 .
drwxr-xr-x  20 sally  staff  680 May 17 08:06 ..
drwxr-xr-x  12 sally  staff  408 May 17 08:07 .git
-rw-r--r--   1 sally  staff  555 May 17 08:07 lottery.c
```

> *Here's another terminology difference with Git. My definition of **pull** is an operation which pulls change-sets into a repository instance but does not update the working copy. **git pull** is equivalent to **pull** followed by **update**. **git fetch** is equivalent to **pull**.*

Now that she has the initial code they had previously discussed, Sally is happy as a horsefly at the church picnic. She wants to check the log to see the details.

```
lottery sally$ git log
commit bcb39bee268a92a6d2930cc8a27ec3402ebecf0d
Author: Harry <harry@futilisoft.com>
Date:   Sat Jun 11 12:55:52 2011 +0200

    initial implementation
```

> *Note the way Git describes this commit: bcb39bee268a.... At the lowest level, a Git version ID is a SHA-1 hash. Git does support various forms of shorthand syntax, including unambiguously shortened SHA-1.*

When Sally decides to take a look at the code, she immediately finds something that makes her nervous as a plump turkey in November. The program expects the red ball number to be the first argument, followed by the other five. But in the actual lottery, the five white numbers are always drawn and shown first. She worries this will be confusing for users so she decides to fix it. Fortunately it is only necessary to modify a few lines of main().

```
if (argc != 7)
{
    fprintf(stderr, "Usage: %s (5 white balls) power_ball\n", argv[0]);
    return -1;
}

int power_ball = atoi(argv[6]);

int white_balls[5];
for (int i=0; i<5; i++)
{
    white_balls[i] = atoi(argv[1+i]);
}
```

Now she uses the **status** operation to see the pending changes.

```
lottery sally$ git status -s
 M lottery.c
```

No surprise there. Git knows that lottery.c has been modified. She wants to double-check by reviewing the actual changes.

```
lottery sally$ git diff
diff --git a/lottery.c b/lottery.c
index e59c732..adf47a7 100644
--- a/lottery.c
+++ b/lottery.c
@@ -11,16 +11,16 @@
 {
     if (argc != 7)
     {
-        fprintf(stderr, "Usage: %s power_ball (5 white balls)\n", argv[0]);
+        fprintf(stderr, "Usage: %s (5 white balls) power_ball\n", argv[0]);
         return -1;
     }

-    int power_ball = atoi(argv[1]);
+    int power_ball = atoi(argv[6]);

     int white_balls[5];
     for (int i=0; i<5; i++)
     {
-        white_balls[i] = atoi(argv[2+i]);
+        white_balls[i] = atoi(argv[1+i]);
     }

     int result = calculate_result(white_balls, power_ball);
```

Ain't that the bee's knees!?!

4. Update, Commit (with a merge)

Meanwhile, Harry has been coding as well. He heard somebody say that it's best to compile with all the warnings turned on, so he decides to give it a try.

```
lottery harry$ gcc -std=c99 -Wall -Wextra -Werror lottery.c
cc1: warnings being treated as errors
lottery.c:5: warning: unused parameter 'white_balls'
lottery.c:5: warning: unused parameter 'power_ball'
```

I say! The code has some warnings. The calculate_result() function isn't using its parameters. Harry looks at the situation and realises the problem immediately: That function should be checking its arguments for validity! The power ball can be from 1 to 39 inclusive. The white balls can be 1 to 59 inclusive. So he implements the error checking.

```
int calculate_result(int white_balls[5], int power_ball)
{
    for (int i=0; i<5; i++)
    {
```

```
        if (
            (white_balls[i] < 1)
            || (white_balls[i] > 59)
          )
        {
            return -1;
        }
    }

    if (
        (power_ball < 1)
        || (power_ball > 39)
      )
    {
        return -1;
    }

    return 0;
}
```

Grand. Let's see if it compiles.

```
lottery harry$ gcc -std=c99 -Wall -Wextra -Werror lottery.c

lottery harry$ ls -l
total 32
-rwxr-xr-x  1 harry  staff  8904 May 17 08:17 a.out
-rw-r--r--  1 harry  staff   843 May 17 08:16 lottery.c
```

Quite. But Harry decides to diff before committing, just for good measure.

```
lottery harry$ git diff
diff --git a/lottery.c b/lottery.c
index e59c732..6b1d76a 100644
--- a/lottery.c
+++ b/lottery.c
@@ -4,6 +4,25 @@

 int calculate_result(int white_balls[5], int power_ball)
 {
+    for (int i=0; i<5; i++)
+    {
+        if (
+            (white_balls[i] < 1)
+            || (white_balls[i] > 59)
+          )
+        {
+            return -1;
+        }
+    }
+
+    if (
+        (power_ball < 1)
```

```
+              || (power_ball > 39)
+         )
+    {
+        return -1;
+    }
+
     return 0;
}
```

Good show. Time to commit the change.

```
lottery harry$ git commit -a -m "fix some warnings"
[master 7895c84] fix some warnings
 1 files changed, 19 insertions(+), 0 deletions(-)
```

No problems there. This time he remembers that he needs to push his changes to the server.

But Sally has been working at the same time and she had her change ready to commit and push first.

```
lottery sally$ git commit -a -m "change order of the command line args to be \
                          more like what the user will expect"
[master 37c09ff] change order of the command line args to be more like what the user ...
 1 files changed, 3 insertions(+), 3 deletions(-)

lottery sally$ git push
Counting objects: 6, done.
Compressing objects: 100% (4/4), done.
Writing objects: 100% (6/6), 397 bytes, done.
Total 6 (delta 1), reused 0 (delta 0)
To http://server.futilisoft.com:8000/lottery
   bcb39be..7895c84  master -> master
```

So Harry tries to push his changes.

```
lottery harry$ git push
To http://server.futilisoft.com:8000/lottery
 ! [rejected]        master -> master (non-fast-forward)
error: failed to push some refs to 'http://server.futilisoft.com:8000/lottery'
To prevent you from losing history, non-fast-forward updates were rejected
Merge the remote changes (e.g. 'git pull') before pushing again.  See the
'Note about fast-forwards' section of 'git push --help' for details.
```

What's all this then? Git is not allowing Harry to push his change because Sally has already pushed something to the master branch.

Harry uses pull to bring in changes.

```
lottery harry$ git pull
remote: Counting objects: 5, done.
remote: Compressing objects: 100% (2/2), done.
remote: Total 3 (delta 1), reused 0 (delta 0)
Unpacking objects: 100% (3/3), done.
From http://server.futilisoft.com:8000/lottery
 + 7895c84...37c09ff master     -> origin/master  (forced update)
Auto-merging lottery.c
Merge made by recursive.
 lottery.c |    6 +++---
 1 files changed, 3 insertions(+), 3 deletions(-)
```

> *I don't like the way Harry did this. He used **git
> pull**, which did the merge and committed it without
> giving Harry a chance to review. Not cool. Harry
> should have used **git pull --no-commit**.*

Now the merge is done.

```
lottery harry$ git status -s
?? a.out
```

Everything seems to be proper good.

```
lottery harry$ git show -c
commit b19f36cf4dddc2f70a597a0b558cf3be3de205b4
Merge: 7895c84 37c09ff
Author: Harry <harry@futilisoft.com>
Date:   Sat Jun 11 14:02:28 2011 +0200

    Merge branch 'master' of http://server.futilisoft.com:8000/lottery

diff --combined lottery.c
index 6b1d76a,adf47a7..22bf053
--- a/lottery.c
+++ b/lottery.c
@@@ -3,25 -3,6 +3,25 @@@

  int calculate_result(int white_balls[5], int power_ball)
  {
+   for (int i=0; i<5; i++)
+   {
+       if (
+           (white_balls[i] < 1)
+           || (white_balls[i] > 59)
```

```
+       )
+       {
+           return -1;
+       }
+   }
+
+   if (
+       (power_ball < 1)
+       || (power_ball > 39)
+       )
+   {
+       return -1;
+   }
+
    return 0;
  }

@@@ -29,16 -10,16 +29,16 @@@ int main(int argc, char** argv
  {
    if (argc != 7)
    {
-       fprintf(stderr, "Usage: %s power_ball (5 white balls)\n", argv[0]);
+       fprintf(stderr, "Usage: %s (5 white balls) power_ball\n", argv[0]);
        return -1;
    }

-   int power_ball = atoi(argv[1]);
+   int power_ball = atoi(argv[6]);

    int white_balls[5];
    for (int i=0; i<5; i++)
    {
-       white_balls[i] = atoi(argv[2+i]);
+       white_balls[i] = atoi(argv[1+i]);
    }

    int result = calculate_result(white_balls, power_ball);
```

The merge commit is done. Apparently Git was able to merge Sally's changes directly into Harry's modified copy of the file without any conflicts. Smashing! Let's see if it compiles.

```
lottery harry$ gcc -std=c99 -Wall -Wextra -Werror lottery.c

lottery harry$ ls -l
total 32
-rwxr-xr-x  1 harry  staff  8904 May 17 08:34 a.out
-rw-r--r--  1 harry  staff   843 May 17 08:28 lottery.c
```

*Harry is checking to see if the merge compiles **after** it has been committed to the repository. If it doesn't compile, he'll need to alter the repository (which Git allows using **git commit --amend**). Git fans love the ability to alter a repository, rearranging things however they want until they push. I understand their perspective and its advantages but I still prefer an approach which treats anything committed to any repository instance as immutable.*

Very well then. So Harry is ready to push the merge.

```
lottery harry$ git push
Counting objects: 10, done.
Compressing objects: 100% (4/4), done.
Writing objects: 100% (6/6), 717 bytes, done.
Total 6 (delta 2), reused 0 (delta 0)
Unpacking objects: 100% (6/6), done.
To http://server.futilisoft.com:8000/lottery
   37c09ff..b19f36c  master -> master
```

5. Update (with merge)

Meanwhile, Sally is fixin' to go ahead and add a feature that was requested by the sales team: If the user chooses the lucky number 7 as the red ball, the chances of winning are doubled. Since she is starting a new task, she decides to begin with pull and update to make sure she has the latest code.

```
lottery sally$ git pull
remote: Counting objects: 10, done.
remote: Compressing objects: 100% (4/4), done.
remote: Total 6 (delta 2), reused 0 (delta 0)
Unpacking objects: 100% (6/6), done.
From http://server.futilisoft.com:8000/lottery
   37c09ff..b19f36c  master      -> origin/master
Updating 37c09ff..b19f36c
Fast-forward
 lottery.c |   19 +++++++++++++++++++
 1 files changed, 19 insertions(+), 0 deletions(-)
```

```
lottery sally$ git show
commit b19f36cf4dddc2f70a597a0b558cf3be3de205b4
Merge: 7895c84 37c09ff
Author: Harry <harry@futilisoft.com>
Date:   Sat Jun 11 14:02:28 2011 +0200

    Merge branch 'master' of http://server.futilisoft.com:8000/lottery
```

Then she implements the lucky 7 feature in two shakes of a lamb's tail by adding just a few lines of new code to main().

```
lottery sally$ git diff
index 22bf053..8548299 100644
--- a/lottery.c
+++ b/lottery.c
@@ -44,6 +44,11 @@

     int result = calculate_result(white_balls, power_ball);

+    if (7 == power_ball)
+    {
+        result = result * 2;
+    }
+
     printf("%d percent chance of winning\n", result);

     return 0;
```

And commits her change. And pushes it too.

```
lottery sally$ git commit -a -m "lucky 7"
[master b77378f] lucky 7
 1 files changed, 5 insertions(+), 0 deletions(-)

lottery sally$ git push
Counting objects: 5, done.
Compressing objects: 100% (2/2), done.
Writing objects: 100% (3/3), 314 bytes, done.
Total 3 (delta 1), reused 0 (delta 0)
Unpacking objects: 100% (3/3), done.
To http://server.futilisoft.com:8000/lottery
   b19f36c..b77378f  master -> master
```

Meanwhile, Harry has realised his last change had a bug. He modified calculate_result() to return -1 for invalid arguments but he forgot to modify the caller to handle the error. As a consequence, entering a ball number that is out of range causes the program to behave improperly.

```
lottery harry$ ./a.out 61 2 3 4 5 42
-1 percent chance of winning
```

The percent chance of winning certainly can't be a negative number, now can it? So Harry adds an extra check for this case.

```
lottery harry$ git diff
diff --git a/lottery.c b/lottery.c
index 22bf053..aad5995 100644
--- a/lottery.c
+++ b/lottery.c
@@ -44,6 +44,12 @@

    int result = calculate_result(white_balls, power_ball);

+    if (result < 0)
+    {
+        fprintf(stderr, "Invalid arguments\n");
+        return -1;
+    }
+
    printf("%d percent chance of winning\n", result);

    return 0;
```

And proceeds to commit and push the fix.

```
lottery harry$ git commit -a -m "propagate error code"
[master 2460684] propagate error code
 1 files changed, 6 insertions(+), 0 deletions(-)

lottery harry$ git push
To http://server.futilisoft.com:8000/lottery
 ! [rejected]        master -> master (non-fast-forward)
error: failed to push some refs to 'http://server.futilisoft.com:8000/lottery'
To prevent you from losing history, non-fast-forward updates were rejected
Merge the remote changes (e.g. 'git pull') before pushing again.  See the
'Note about fast-forwards' section of 'git push --help' for details.
.
```

Blimey! Sally must have pushed a new changeset already. Harry once again needs to pull and merge to combine Sally's changes with his own.

```
lottery harry$ git pull
remote: Counting objects: 5, done.
remote: Compressing objects: 100% (2/2), done.
remote: Total 3 (delta 1), reused 0 (delta 0)
Unpacking objects: 100% (3/3), done.
From http://server.futilisoft.com:8000/lottery
   b19f36c..b77378f  master       -> origin/master
Auto-merging lottery.c
CONFLICT (content): Merge conflict in lottery.c
Automatic merge failed; fix conflicts and then commit the result.
```

The merge didn't go quite as smoothly this time. Harry wonders if anyone would notice if he were to sneak off to the pub. Apparently there was a conflict. Harry decides to open up lottery.c in his editor to examine the situation.

```
...
    int result = calculate_result(white_balls, power_ball);
<<<<<<< HEAD
    if (result < 0)
    {
        fprintf(stderr, "Invalid arguments\n");
        return -1;
=======
    if (7 == power_ball)
    {
        result = result * 2;
>>>>>>> b77378f6eb0af44468be36a085c3fe06a80e0322
    }

    printf("%d percent chance of winning\n", result);

    return 0;
...
```

Git has included both Harry's code and Sally's code with conflict markers to delimit things. What we want is to include both blocks of code. Sally's new code can simply be included right after Harry's error checking.

```
...
    int result = calculate_result(white_balls, power_ball);

    if (result < 0)
    {
        fprintf(stderr, "Invalid arguments\n");
        return -1;
    }

    if (7 == power_ball)
    {
        result = result * 2;
    }

    printf("%d percent chance of winning\n", result);

    return 0;
...
```

That should take care of the problem. Harry compiles the code to make sure and then commits the merge.

```
lottery harry$ git status -s
UU lottery.c
?? a.out

lottery harry$ git status
# On branch master
# Your branch and 'origin/master' have diverged,
# and have 1 and 1 different commit(s) each, respectively.
#
# Unmerged paths:
#   (use "git add/rm <file>..." as appropriate to mark resolution)
#
#       both modified:      lottery.c
#
# Untracked files:
#   (use "git add <file>..." to include in what will be committed)
#
#       a.out
no changes added to commit (use "git add" and/or "git commit -a")
```

```
lottery harry$ git commit -a -m "merge"
[master 05f316d] merge
```

And then to retry the push.

```
lottery harry$ git push
Counting objects: 10, done.
Compressing objects: 100% (4/4), done.
Writing objects: 100% (6/6), 573 bytes, done.
Total 6 (delta 2), reused 0 (delta 0)
Unpacking objects: 100% (6/6), done.
To http://server.futilisoft.com:8000/lottery
   b77378f..05f316d  master -> master
```

And… that's the last wicket.

6. Move

Harry immediately moves on to his next task, which is to restructure the tree a bit. He doesn't want the top level of the repository to get too cluttered so he decides to move their vast number of source code files into a src subdirectory.

```
lottery harry$ mkdir src

lottery harry$ git mv lottery.c src

lottery harry$ git status -s
```

```
R  lottery.c -> src/lottery.c
?? a.out

lottery harry$ git commit -a -m "dir structure"
[master 0171af4] dir structure
 1 files changed, 0 insertions(+), 0 deletions(-)
 rename lottery.c => src/lottery.c (100%)

lottery harry$ git push
Counting objects: 3, done.
Writing objects: 100% (2/2), 223 bytes, done.
Total 2 (delta 0), reused 0 (delta 0)
Unpacking objects: 100% (2/2), done.
To http://server.futilisoft.com:8000/lottery
   05f316d..0171af4  master -> master
```

Having the number 7 as a constant in the code is so ugly it makes Sally's hair hurt. She adds a #define to give it a more meaningful name.

```
lottery sally$ git diff
diff --git a/lottery.c b/lottery.c
index 8548299..cf21604 100644
--- a/lottery.c
+++ b/lottery.c
@@ -2,6 +2,8 @@
 #include <stdio.h>
 #include <stdlib.h>

+#define LUCKY_NUMBER 7
+
 int calculate_result(int white_balls[5], int power_ball)
 {
     for (int i=0; i<5; i++)
@@ -50,7 +52,7 @@
         return -1;
     }

-    if (7 == power_ball)
+    if (LUCKY_NUMBER == power_ball)
     {
         result = result * 2;
     }
```

And immediately commits and pushes the change.

```
lottery sally$ git commit -a -m "use a #define for the lucky number"
[master f3988a0] use a #define for the lucky number
 1 files changed, 3 insertions(+), 1 deletions(-)

lottery sally$ git push
To http://server.futilisoft.com:8000/lottery
 ! [rejected]        master -> master (non-fast-forward)
```

```
error: failed to push some refs to 'http://server.futilisoft.com:8000/lottery'
To prevent you from losing history, non-fast-forward updates were rejected
Merge the remote changes (e.g. 'git pull') before pushing again.  See the
'Note about fast-forwards' section of 'git push --help' for details.
```

Hmmm. Sally needs to pull and merge before she can push her changes.

```
lottery sally$ git pull
remote: Counting objects: 12, done.
remote: Compressing objects: 100% (5/5), done.
remote: Total 8 (delta 1), reused 0 (delta 0)
Unpacking objects: 100% (8/8), done.
From http://server.futilisoft.com:8000/lottery
   b77378f..0171af4  master      -> origin/master
Auto-merging src/lottery.c
CONFLICT (content): Merge conflict in src/lottery.c
Automatic merge failed; fix conflicts and then commit the result.
```

Let's see what the conflict is:

```
lottery sally$ git diff
diff --cc src/lottery.c
index cf21604,49c6688..0000000
--- a/src/lottery.c
+++ b/src/lottery.c
@@@ -45,7 -43,13 +45,17 @@@ int main(int argc, char** argv

     int result = calculate_result(white_balls, power_ball);

++<<<<<<< HEAD
 +  if (LUCKY_NUMBER == power_ball)
++=======
+   if (result < 0)
+   {
+       fprintf(stderr, "Invalid arguments\n");
+       return -1;
+   }
+
+   if (7 == power_ball)
++>>>>>>> 0171af4004103031d2ffb8d26fac0bcc9511060d
    {
        result = result * 2;
    }
```

She sees that the problem is easy to resolve.

```
lottery sally$ git diff
diff --cc src/lottery.c
index cf21604,49c6688..0000000
--- a/src/lottery.c
+++ b/src/lottery.c
```

```
@@@ -45,7 -43,13 +45,13 @@@ int main(int argc, char** argv

    int result = calculate_result(white_balls, power_ball);

+   if (result < 0)
+   {
+       fprintf(stderr, "Invalid arguments\n");
+       return -1;
+   }
+
-   if (7 == power_ball)
+   if (LUCKY_NUMBER == power_ball)
    {
        result = result * 2;
    }
```

And commits and pushes the change.

```
lottery sally$ git commit -a -m "merge"
[master 0e74df9] merge

lottery sally$ git push
Counting objects: 12, done.
Compressing objects: 100% (4/4), done.
Writing objects: 100% (7/7), 602 bytes, done.
Total 7 (delta 2), reused 0 (delta 0)
Unpacking objects: 100% (7/7), done.
To http://server.futilisoft.com:8000/lottery
   0171af4..0e74df9  master -> master
```

7. Rename

Harry decides the time has come to create a proper Makefile. And also to gratuitously rename lottery.c.

```
lottery harry$ git pull
remote: Counting objects: 12, done.
remote: Compressing objects: 100% (4/4), done.
remote: Total 7 (delta 2), reused 0 (delta 0)
Unpacking objects: 100% (7/7), done.
From http://server.futilisoft.com:8000/lottery
   0171af4..0e74df9  master       -> origin/master
Updating 0171af4..0e74df9
Fast-forward
 src/lottery.c |    4 +++-
 1 files changed, 3 insertions(+), 1 deletions(-)

lottery harry$ git add Makefile

lottery harry$ git mv src/lottery.c src/pb.c
```

```
lottery harry$ git status -s
A  Makefile
R  src/lottery.c -> src/pb.c
?? a.out

lottery harry$ git commit -a -m "Makefile. and lottery.c was too long to type."
[master 8e9cb1b] Makefile. and lottery.c was too long to type.
 2 files changed, 4 insertions(+), 0 deletions(-)
 create mode 100644 Makefile
 rename src/{lottery.c => pb.c} (100%)

lottery harry$ git push
Counting objects: 6, done.
Compressing objects: 100% (3/3), done.
Writing objects: 100% (4/4), 399 bytes, done.
Total 4 (delta 0), reused 0 (delta 0)
Unpacking objects: 100% (4/4), done.
To http://server.futilisoft.com:8000/lottery
   0e74df9..8e9cb1b  master -> master
```

Sally maintains her momentum with #define and adds names for the ball ranges.

```
lottery sally$ git diff
diff --git a/src/lottery.c b/src/lottery.c
index 706851c..9f3ce49 100644
--- a/src/lottery.c
+++ b/src/lottery.c
@@ -3,6 +3,8 @@
 #include <stdlib.h>

 #define LUCKY_NUMBER 7
+#define MAX_WHITE_BALL 59
+#define MAX_POWER_BALL 39

 int calculate_result(int white_balls[5], int power_ball)
 {
@@ -10,7 +12,7 @@
     {
         if (
             (white_balls[i] < 1)
-            || (white_balls[i] > 59)
+            || (white_balls[i] > MAX_WHITE_BALL)
         )
         {
             return -1;
@@ -19,7 +21,7 @@

     if (
         (power_ball < 1)
-        || (power_ball > 39)
```

```
+            || (power_ball > MAX_POWER_BALL)
       )
    {
       return -1;
```

And commits her changes.

```
lottery sally$ git commit -a -m "more #defines"
[master 933ffc3] more #defines
 1 files changed, 4 insertions(+), 2 deletions(-)

lottery sally$ git push
To http://server.futilisoft.com:8000/lottery
 ! [rejected]        master -> master (non-fast-forward)
error: failed to push some refs to 'http://server.futilisoft.com:8000/lottery'
To prevent you from losing history, non-fast-forward updates were rejected
Merge the remote changes (e.g. 'git pull') before pushing again.  See the
'Note about fast-forwards' section of 'git push --help' for details.
```

Grrr. That Harry. The brain in his head must be like a BB in a boxcar.

```
lottery sally$ git pull
remote: Counting objects: 6, done.
remote: Compressing objects: 100% (3/3), done.
remote: Total 4 (delta 0), reused 0 (delta 0)
Unpacking objects: 100% (4/4), done.
From http://server.futilisoft.com:8000/lottery
   0e74df9..8e9cb1b  master     -> origin/master
Merge made by recursive.
 Makefile              |    4 ++++
 src/{lottery.c => pb.c} |    0
 2 files changed, 4 insertions(+), 0 deletions(-)
 create mode 100644 Makefile
 rename src/{lottery.c => pb.c} (100%)

lottery sally$ make
gcc -std=c99 -Wall -Wextra -Werror src/pb.c -o pb

lottery sally$ git push
Counting objects: 12, done.
Compressing objects: 100% (4/4), done.
Writing objects: 100% (7/7), 696 bytes, done.
Total 7 (delta 1), reused 0 (delta 0)
Unpacking objects: 100% (7/7), done.
To http://server.futilisoft.com:8000/lottery
   8e9cb1b..00b1b4f  master -> master
```

8. Delete

Harry wants to get a head start on Zawinski's Law, so he decides to add an IMAP protocol library to their tree.

```
lottery harry$ git pull
remote: Counting objects: 12, done.
remote: Compressing objects: 100% (4/4), done.
remote: Total 7 (delta 1), reused 0 (delta 0)
Unpacking objects: 100% (7/7), done.
From http://server.futilisoft.com:8000/lottery
   8e9cb1b..00b1b4f  master     -> origin/master
Updating 8e9cb1b..00b1b4f
Fast-forward
 src/pb.c |    6 ++++--
 1 files changed, 4 insertions(+), 2 deletions(-)

lottery harry$ git add -v libvmime-0.9.1
add 'libvmime-0.9.1/AUTHORS'
add 'libvmime-0.9.1/COPYING'
add 'libvmime-0.9.1/ChangeLog'
add 'libvmime-0.9.1/HACKING'
add 'libvmime-0.9.1/INSTALL'
add 'libvmime-0.9.1/Makefile.am'
...

lottery harry$ git commit -a -m "add libvmime so we can do the mail reader feature"
[master 5b8342b] add libvmime so we can do the mail reader feature
 443 files changed, 45673 insertions(+), 0 deletions(-)
 create mode 100644 libvmime-0.9.1/AUTHORS
 create mode 100644 libvmime-0.9.1/COPYING
 create mode 100644 libvmime-0.9.1/ChangeLog
 create mode 100644 libvmime-0.9.1/HACKING
 create mode 100644 libvmime-0.9.1/INSTALL
 create mode 100644 libvmime-0.9.1/Makefile.am
...

lottery harry$ git push
Counting objects: 5, done.
Compressing objects: 100% (3/3), done.
Writing objects: 100% (4/4), 446 bytes, done.
Total 4 (delta 0), reused 0 (delta 0)
Unpacking objects: 100% (4/4), done.
To http://server.futilisoft.com:8000/lottery
   00b1b4f..3e04765  master -> master
```

Sally does a pull and finds something only a little better than a sharp stick in the eye.

```
lottery sally$ git pull
remote: Counting objects: 5, done.
remote: Compressing objects: 100% (3/3), done.
remote: Total 4 (delta 0), reused 0 (delta 0)
```

```
Unpacking objects: 100% (4/4), done.
From http://server.futilisoft.com:8000/lottery
   00b1b4f..3e04765  master      -> origin/master
Updating 00b1b4f..3e04765
Fast-forward
 443 files changed, 45673 insertions(+), 0 deletions(-)
 create mode 100644 libvmime-0.9.1/AUTHORS
 create mode 100644 libvmime-0.9.1/COPYING
 create mode 100644 libvmime-0.9.1/ChangeLog
 create mode 100644 libvmime-0.9.1/HACKING
 create mode 100644 libvmime-0.9.1/INSTALL
 create mode 100644 libvmime-0.9.1/Makefile.am
...
```

Sally remembers that the specification says the product isn't supposed to include a full email reader until the next release. For the entire 1.0 development cycle, that third party library is going to be about as useful as socks on a rooster. So she deletes it.

```
lottery sally$ git rm libvmime-0.9.1
fatal: not removing 'libvmime-0.9.1' recursively without -r

lottery sally$ git rm -r libvmime-0.9.1
rm 'libvmime-0.9.1/AUTHORS'
rm 'libvmime-0.9.1/COPYING'
rm 'libvmime-0.9.1/ChangeLog'
rm 'libvmime-0.9.1/HACKING'
rm 'libvmime-0.9.1/INSTALL'
rm 'libvmime-0.9.1/Makefile.am'
...

lottery sally$ git commit -a -m "no mail reader until 2.0"
[master 3cdcf54] no mail reader until 2.0
 443 files changed, 0 insertions(+), 45673 deletions(-)
 delete mode 100644 libvmime-0.9.1/
 delete mode 100644 libvmime-0.9.1/AUTHORS
 delete mode 100644 libvmime-0.9.1/COPYING
 delete mode 100644 libvmime-0.9.1/ChangeLog
 delete mode 100644 libvmime-0.9.1/HACKING
 delete mode 100644 libvmime-0.9.1/INSTALL
 delete mode 100644 libvmime-0.9.1/Makefile.am
...

lottery sally$ git push
Counting objects: 3, done.
Compressing objects: 100% (2/2), done.
Writing objects: 100% (2/2), 267 bytes, done.
Total 2 (delta 0), reused 0 (delta 0)
Unpacking objects: 100% (2/2), done.
To http://server.futilisoft.com:8000/lottery
   3e04765..3cdcf54  master -> master
```

9. Revert

Harry updates his repository instance.

```
lottery harry$ git pull
remote: Counting objects: 3, done.
remote: Compressing objects: 100% (2/2), done.
Unpacking objects: 100% (2/2), done.
remote: Total 2 (delta 0), reused 0 (delta 0)
From http://server.futilisoft.com:8000/lottery
   3e04765..3cdcf54  master     -> origin/master
Updating 3e04765..3cdcf54
Fast-forward
 443 files changed, 0 insertions(+), 45673 deletions(-)
 delete mode 100644 libvmime-0.9.1/
 delete mode 100644 libvmime-0.9.1/AUTHORS
 delete mode 100644 libvmime-0.9.1/COPYING
 delete mode 100644 libvmime-0.9.1/ChangeLog
 delete mode 100644 libvmime-0.9.1/HACKING
 delete mode 100644 libvmime-0.9.1/INSTALL
 delete mode 100644 libvmime-0.9.1/Makefile.am
...

lottery harry$ ls -l
total 8
-rw-r--r-- 1 harry staff  66 May 17 11:47 Makefile
drwxr-xr-x 3 harry staff 102 May 17 13:58 src
```

Sod it! That Sally must be barmy! She's deleted all his email code! Harry decides to indent[2] pb.c.

```
lottery harry$ indent src/pb.c

lottery harry$ git status -s
 M src/pb.c
? pb.c.BAK
```

Harry whinges for a while, calms down and reverts the changes.

---

[2]http://en.wikipedia.org/wiki/Indent_(Unix)

```
lottery harry$ git checkout src/pb.c

lottery harry$ git status -s
?? pb.c.BAK

lottery harry$ rm pb.c.BAK

lottery harry$ git status -s

lottery harry$ git status
# On branch master
nothing to commit (working directory clean)
```

> *Git doesn't exactly have a **revert** command. Or rather, it does, but **git revert** does something else, not what I call **revert**. To revert the contents of a file, Harry uses **git checkout filename**.*

Sally has decided to eliminate uses of atoi(), which is deprecated.

```
lottery sally$ git diff
diff --git a/src/pb.c b/src/pb.c
index 9f3ce49..cd378f5 100644
--- a/src/pb.c
+++ b/src/pb.c
@@ -43,7 +43,14 @@
     int white_balls[5];
     for (int i=0; i<5; i++)
     {
-        white_balls[i] = atoi(argv[1+i]);
+        char* endptr = NULL;
+        long val = strtol(argv[1+i], &endptr, 10);
+        if (*endptr)
+        {
+            fprintf(stderr, "Invalid arguments\n");
+            return -1;
+        }
+        white_balls[i] = (int) val;
     }

     int result = calculate_result(white_balls, power_ball);

lottery sally$ make
gcc -std=c99 -Wall -Wextra -Werror pb.c -o pb

lottery sally$ ./pb 1 2 3 4 5 6
```

```
0 percent chance of winning

lottery sally$ ./pb 1 2 3e 4 5 6
Invalid arguments
```

And she commits her changes, easy as slipping in the mud.

```
lottery sally$ git commit -a -m "use strtol. atoi is deprecated."
[master 4c75c49] use strtol. atoi is deprecated.
 1 files changed, 8 insertions(+), 1 deletions(-)

lottery sally$ git push
Counting objects: 7, done.
Compressing objects: 100% (3/3), done.
Writing objects: 100% (4/4), 463 bytes, done.
Total 4 (delta 1), reused 0 (delta 0)
Unpacking objects: 100% (4/4), done.
To http://server.futilisoft.com:8000/lottery
   3cdcf54..4c75c49  master -> master
```

10. Tag

Still mourning the loss of his email code, Harry creates a tag so he can more easily access it later.

```
lottery harry$ git log
...
commit 3e047651520a0232dcb7385d79962e04d529934b
Author: Harry <harry@futilisoft.com>
Date:   Sat Jun 11 16:17:11 2011 +0200

    add libvmime so we can do the mail reader feature
...

lottery harry$ git tag just_before_sally_deleted_my_email_code 3e047651

lottery harry$ git tag
just_before_sally_deleted_my_email_code

lottery harry$ git log --decorate
commit 3cdcf5424d79aeebd28fd40e54465914d8a4a73d (HEAD, origin/master, master)
Author: Sally <sally@futilisoft.com>
Date:   Sat Jun 11 16:23:16 2011 +0200

    no mail reader until 2.0

commit 3e047651520a0232dcb7385d79962e04d529934b (tag: just_before_sally_...
Author: Harry <harry@futilisoft.com>
```

```
Date:   Sat Jun 11 16:17:11 2011 +0200

    add libvmime so we can do the mail reader feature
...
```

Harry wants to share his misery, so he pushes the tag.

```
lottery harry$ git push origin tag just_before_sally_deleted_my_email_code
Counting objects: 45, done.
Compressing objects: 100% (29/29), done.
Writing objects: 100% (45/45), 4.19 KiB, done.
Total 45 (delta 9), reused 0 (delta 0)
Unpacking objects: 100% (45/45), done.
To http://server.futilisoft.com:8000/lottery
 * [new tag]           just_before_sally_deleted_my_email_code -> just_before_sally_...
```

Sally sees Harry gloating in the company chat room about his beloved tag, so she wants to see what he did.

```
lottery sally$ git pull
From http://server.futilisoft.com:8000/lottery
 * [new tag]           just_before_sally_deleted_my_email_code -> just_before_sally_...
Already up-to-date.
```

Sally sees Harry's tag and rolls her eyes. Fine. Whatever.

11. Branch

Sally wants more privacy. She decides to create her own named branch.

```
lottery sally$ git checkout -b no_boys_allowed
Switched to a new branch 'no_boys_allowed'
```

Now that Sally is working in her own branch, she feels much more productive. She adds support for the "favorite" option. When a user is playing her favorite numbers, her chances of winning should be doubled. In doing this, she had to rework the way command-line args are parsed. And she removes an atoi() call she missed last time. And she restructures all the error checking into one place.

So main() now looks like this:

```
int main(int argc, char** argv)
{
    int balls[6];
    int count_balls = 0;
```

```c
int favorite = 0;

for (int i=1; i<argc; i++)
{
    const char* arg = argv[i];

    if ('-' == arg[0])
    {
        if (0 == strcmp(arg, "-favorite"))
        {
            favorite = 1;
        }
        else
        {
            goto usage_error;
        }
    }
    else
    {
        char* endptr = NULL;
        long val = strtol(arg, &endptr, 10);
        if (*endptr)
        {
            goto usage_error;
        }
        balls[count_balls++] = (int) val;
    }
}

if (6 != count_balls)
{
    goto usage_error;
}

int power_ball = balls[5];

int result = calculate_result(balls, power_ball);

if (result < 0)
{
    goto usage_error;
}

if (LUCKY_NUMBER == power_ball)
{
    result = result * 2;
}

if (favorite)
{
    result = result * 2;
}

printf("%d percent chance of winning\n", result);
```

```
      return 0;

usage_error:
    fprintf(stderr, "Usage: %s [-favorite] (5 white balls) power_ball\n", argv[0]);
    return -1;
}
```

She commits her changes, knowing that the commit will succeed because she is working in her private branch.

```
lottery sally$ git commit -a -m "add -favorite and cleanup some other stuff"
[no_boys_allowed 02f9797] add -favorite and cleanup some other stuff
 1 files changed, 43 insertions(+), 18 deletions(-)

lottery sally$ git push
Everything up-to-date
```

Hey! What's the problem here? Ah, Git just wants Sally to be more explicit about the fact that she's pushing a new branch.

```
lottery sally$ git push origin no_boys_allowed
Counting objects: 7, done.
Compressing objects: 100% (3/3), done.
Writing objects: 100% (4/4), 705 bytes, done.
Total 4 (delta 1), reused 0 (delta 0)
Unpacking objects: 100% (4/4), done.
To http://server.futilisoft.com:8000/lottery
 * [new branch]      no_boys_allowed -> no_boys_allowed
```

12. Merge (no conflicts)

Meanwhile, over in the default branch, Harry decides the white balls should be sorted before analysing them, because that's how they are on the telly.

```
lottery harry$ git diff
diff --git a/src/pb.c b/src/pb.c
index 9f3ce49..45c5730 100644
--- a/src/pb.c
+++ b/src/pb.c
@@ -6,6 +6,25 @@
 #define MAX_WHITE_BALL 59
 #define MAX_POWER_BALL 39

+static int my_sort_func(const void* p1, const void* p2)
+{
+    int v1 = *((int *) p1);
+    int v2 = *((int *) p2);
+
```

```
+    if (v1 < v2)
+    {
+        return -1;
+    }
+    else if (v1 > v2)
+    {
+        return 1;
+    }
+    else
+    {
+        return 0;
+    }
+}
+
 int calculate_result(int white_balls[5], int power_ball)
 {
     for (int i=0; i<5; i++)
@@ -27,6 +46,8 @@
         return -1;
     }

+    qsort(white_balls, 5, sizeof(int), my_sort_func);
+
     return 0;
 }

lottery harry$ git commit -a -m "sort the white balls"
[master eabf466] sort the white balls
 1 files changed, 20 insertions(+), 0 deletions(-)
```

But now he's curious about what Sally has been doing. She said he wasn't allowed to commit to her branch but she didn't say anything about **looking** at it.

```
lottery harry$ git fetch
remote: Counting objects: 11, done.
remote: Compressing objects: 100% (6/6), done.
remote: Total 8 (delta 2), reused 0 (delta 0)
Unpacking objects: 100% (8/8), done.
From http://server.futilisoft.com:8000/lottery
 * [new branch]      no_boys_allowed -> origin/no_boys_allowed

lottery harry$ git log ..origin/no_boys_allowed
commit 02f97979589ee827dfa3f4cfb662eb246b48d919
Author: Sally <sally@futilisoft.com>
Date:   Sat Jun 11 17:55:35 2011 +0200

    add -favorite and cleanup some other stuff
```

Interesting. She added the "favorite" feature. Harry decides he wants that. So he asks Git to merge stuff from Sally's branch into the default branch.

```
lottery harry$ git merge origin/no_boys_allowed
Auto-merging src/pb.c
Merge made by recursive.
 src/pb.c |   61 +++++++++++++++++++++++++++++++++++++++++++-------------------
 1 files changed, 43 insertions(+), 18 deletions(-)
```

Brilliant! Harry examines pb.c and discovers that it was merged correctly. Sally's "favorite" changes are there and his qsort changes are as well. So he compiles the code, runs a quick test, and commits the merge.

```
lottery harry$ make
gcc -std=c99 -Wall -Wextra -Werror pb.c -o pb

lottery harry$ ./pb -favorite 5 3 33 22 7 31
0 percent chance of winning

lottery harry$ git push
Counting objects: 14, done.
Compressing objects: 100% (6/6), done.
Writing objects: 100% (8/8), 1.06 KiB, done.
Total 8 (delta 2), reused 0 (delta 0)
Unpacking objects: 100% (8/8), done.
To http://server.futilisoft.com:8000/lottery
   4c75c49..df43333  master -> master
```

13. Merge (repeated, no conflicts)

Simultaneously, both Harry and Sally realize that their code has no comments.

Harry:

```
lottery harry$ git diff
diff --git a/src/pb.c b/src/pb.c
index 961c1f2..f7d0b61 100644
--- a/src/pb.c
+++ b/src/pb.c
@@ -47,6 +47,7 @@
        return -1;
    }

+   // lottery ball numbers are always shown sorted
    qsort(white_balls, 5, sizeof(int), my_sort_func);

    return 0;

lottery harry$ git commit -a -m comments
[master 571e482] comments
 1 files changed, 1 insertions(+), 0 deletions(-)
```

```
lottery harry$ git push
Counting objects: 7, done.
Compressing objects: 100% (3/3), done.
Writing objects: 100% (4/4), 388 bytes, done.
Total 4 (delta 1), reused 0 (delta 0)
Unpacking objects: 100% (4/4), done.
To http://server.futilisoft.com:8000/lottery
   df43333..571e482  master -> master
```

And Sally:

```
lottery sally$ git diff
diff --git a/src/pb.c b/src/pb.c
index ad680c7..7881352 100644
--- a/src/pb.c
+++ b/src/pb.c
@@ -35,7 +35,7 @@
 {
     int balls[6];
     int count_balls = 0;
-    int favorite = 0;
+    int favorite = 0;  // this should be a bool

     for (int i=1; i<argc; i++)
     {
@@ -69,10 +69,13 @@
         goto usage_error;
     }

+    // the power ball is always the last one given
     int power_ball = balls[5];

     int result = calculate_result(balls, power_ball);

+    // calculate result can return -1 if the ball numbers
+    // are out of range
     if (result < 0)
     {
         goto usage_error;

lottery sally$ git commit -a -m comments
[no_boys_allowed 7570e84] comments
 1 files changed, 4 insertions(+), 1 deletions(-)

lottery sally$ git push
Counting objects: 7, done.
Compressing objects: 100% (3/3), done.
Writing objects: 100% (4/4), 474 bytes, done.
Total 4 (delta 1), reused 0 (delta 0)
Unpacking objects: 100% (4/4), done.
To http://server.futilisoft.com:8000/lottery
   02f9797..7570e84  no_boys_allowed -> no_boys_allowed
 ! [rejected]        master -> master (non-fast-forward)
```

```
error: failed to push some refs to 'http://server.futilisoft.com:8000/lottery'
To prevent you from losing history, non-fast-forward updates were rejected
Merge the remote changes (e.g. 'git pull') before pushing again.  See the
'Note about fast-forwards' section of 'git push --help' for details.
```

Sally notices that the push of her private branch succeeded. Git seems to be griping about something else, related to the master branch. She thinks it best that she just ignore it.

> *That error message is Git's way of saying the master branch in Sally's repository instance is out of date.*

Harry decides to try again to merge the changes from Sally's branch.

```
lottery harry$ git pull
remote: Counting objects: 7, done.
remote: Compressing objects: 100% (3/3), done.
remote: Total 4 (delta 1), reused 0 (delta 0)
Unpacking objects: 100% (4/4), done.
From http://server.futilisoft.com:8000/lottery
   02f9797..7570e84  no_boys_allowed -> origin/no_boys_allowed
Already up-to-date.

lottery harry$ git merge origin/no_boys_allowed
Auto-merging src/pb.c
Merge made by recursive.
 src/pb.c |    5 ++++-
 1 files changed, 4 insertions(+), 1 deletions(-)
```

No worries on the merge then. Harry checks to see if everything compiles.

```
lottery harry$ make
gcc -std=c99 -Wall -Wextra -Werror pb.c -o pb

lottery harry$ git push
Counting objects: 10, done.
Compressing objects: 100% (3/3), done.
Unpacking objects: 100% (4/4), done.
Writing objects: 100% (4/4), 541 bytes, done.
Total 4 (delta 1), reused 0 (delta 0)
To http://server.futilisoft.com:8000/lottery
   571e482..31b9ef7  master -> master
```

14. Merge (conflicts)

Sally realizes that C99 has a bool type that should have been used.

```
lottery sally$ git diff
diff --git a/src/pb.c b/src/pb.c
index 7881352..3351455 100644
--- a/src/pb.c
+++ b/src/pb.c
@@ -2,6 +2,7 @@
 #include <stdio.h>
 #include <stdlib.h>
 #include <string.h>
+#include <stdbool.h>

 #define LUCKY_NUMBER 7
 #define MAX_WHITE_BALL 59
@@ -35,7 +36,7 @@
 {
     int balls[6];
     int count_balls = 0;
-    int favorite = 0;  // this should be a bool
+    bool favorite = false;

     for (int i=1; i<argc; i++)
     {
@@ -45,7 +46,7 @@
         {
             if (0 == strcmp(arg, "-favorite"))
             {
-                favorite = 1;
+                favorite = true;
             }
             else
             {
```

And she commits the change to her private branch.

```
lottery sally$ git commit -a -m "use the bool type"
[no_boys_allowed a1d4dcf] use the bool type
 1 files changed, 4 insertions(+), 2 deletions(-)

lottery sally$ git push origin HEAD
Counting objects: 7, done.
Compressing objects: 100% (3/3), done.
Writing objects: 100% (4/4), 406 bytes, done.
Total 4 (delta 1), reused 0 (delta 0)
Unpacking objects: 100% (4/4), done.
To http://server.futilisoft.com:8000/lottery
   7570e84..a1d4dcf  HEAD -> no_boys_allowed
```

Meanwhile, Harry has been grumbling about Sally's butchering of the Queen's English and decides to correct the spelling of the word "favourite".

```
lottery harry$ git diff
diff --git a/src/pb.c b/src/pb.c
index 0cecd1c..4d28bbb 100644
--- a/src/pb.c
+++ b/src/pb.c
@@ -57,7 +57,7 @@
 {
     int balls[6];
     int count_balls = 0;
-    int favorite = 0;  // this should be a bool
+    int favourite = 0;  // this should be a bool

     for (int i=1; i<argc; i++)
     {
@@ -65,9 +65,9 @@

         if ('-' == arg[0])
         {
-            if (0 == strcmp(arg, "-favorite"))
+            if (0 == strcmp(arg, "-favourite"))
             {
-                favorite = 1;
+                favourite = 1;
             }
             else
             {
@@ -108,7 +108,7 @@
         result = result * 2;
     }

-    if (favorite)
+    if (favourite)
     {
         result = result * 2;
     }
@@ -118,7 +118,7 @@
     return 0;

 usage_error:
-    fprintf(stderr, "Usage: %s [-favorite] (5 white balls) power_ball\n", argv[0]);
+    fprintf(stderr, "Usage: %s [-favourite] (5 white balls) power_ball\n", argv[0]);
     return -1;
 }
```

Feeling quite chuffed about his pedantry, Harry proceeds to commit the change.

```
lottery harry$ git commit -a -m "fixed spelling error"
[master f822657] fixed spelling error
 1 files changed, 5 insertions(+), 5 deletions(-)
```

And to once again merge Sally's changes into the default branch.

```
lottery harry$ git fetch
remote: Counting objects: 7, done.
remote: Compressing objects: 100% (3/3), done.
remote: Total 4 (delta 1), reused 0 (delta 0)
Unpacking objects: 100% (4/4), done.
From http://server.futilisoft.com:8000/lottery
   7570e84..a1d4dcf  no_boys_allowed -> origin/no_boys_allowed

lottery harry$ git merge origin/no_boys_allowed
Auto-merging src/pb.c
CONFLICT (content): Merge conflict in src/pb.c
Automatic merge failed; fix conflicts and then commit the result.
```

Crikey! Conflicts in pb.c again.

```
lottery harry$ git diff
diff --cc src/pb.c
index 4d28bbb,3351455..0000000
--- a/src/pb.c
+++ b/src/pb.c
@@@ -1,6 -1,7 +1,10 @@@
  #include <stdio.h>
  #include <stdlib.h>
  #include <string.h>
++<<<<<<< HEAD
++=======
+ #include <stdbool.h>
++>>>>>>> origin/no_boys_allowed

  #define LUCKY_NUMBER 7
  #define MAX_WHITE_BALL 59
@@@ -55,7 -35,7 +59,11 @@@ int main(int argc, char** argv
  {
    int balls[6];
    int count_balls = 0;
++<<<<<<< HEAD
 +  int favourite = 0; // this should be a bool
++=======
+   bool favorite = false;
++>>>>>>> origin/no_boys_allowed

    for (int i=1; i<argc; i++)
    {
@@@ -63,9 -43,9 +71,13 @@@

      if ('-' == arg[0])
      {
 -         if (0 == strcmp(arg, "-favorite"))
 +         if (0 == strcmp(arg, "-favourite"))
          {
++<<<<<<< HEAD
```

```
+                    favourite = 1;
++=======
+                    favorite = true;
++>>>>>>> origin/no_boys_allowed
            }
            else
            {
```

That **is** a sticky wicket. Harry quickly realises this conflict needs to be resolved manually by keeping the proper spelling but converting the type to bool like Sally did.

```
lottery harry$ git diff
diff --cc src/pb.c
index 4d28bbb,3351455..0000000
--- a/src/pb.c
+++ b/src/pb.c
@@@ -55,7 -35,7 +56,7 @@@ int main(int argc, char** argv
   {
     int balls[6];
     int count_balls = 0;
-    int favourite = 0; // this should be a bool
 -   bool favorite = false;
++    bool favourite = false;

     for (int i=1; i<argc; i++)
     {
@@@ -63,9 -43,9 +64,9 @@@

         if ('-' == arg[0])
         {
-            if (0 == strcmp(arg, "-favorite"))
+            if (0 == strcmp(arg, "-favourite"))
             {
-                favourite = 1;
 -               favorite = true;
++                favourite = true;
             }
             else
             {
```

After manually merging the changes, Harry proceeds to resolve the conflict and commit the merge.

```
lottery harry$ git commit -a -m "merge, conflicts fixed"
[master b5480ab] merge, conflicts fixed

lottery harry$ git push
...
```

And all of Futilisoft's customers lived happily ever after.

15. Summary

The following table summarizes all 21 commands for Git. See Table A.1 in Appendix A for a comparison of Git's commands with other tools.

Operation	Git Command
Create	git init
Checkout	a
Commit	git commit -a [b]
Update	git checkout [c]
Add	git add [d]
Edit	git add [e]
Delete	git rm
Rename	git mv
Move	git mv
Status	git status
Diff	git diff
Revert	git checkout [f]
Log	git log
Tag	git tag
Branch	git branch
Merge	git merge
Resolve	g
Lock	h
Clone	git clone
Push	git push
Pull	git fetch [i]

[a] N/A: Git keeps the repository instance inside the working copy.

[b] Without the -a flag, git will commit only those changes which have been explicitly added to its *staging area*.

[c] Git automatically updates the working copy as part of a **git pull**.

[d] **git add** is also used to add any sort of change to the staging area.

[e] Or use **git commit -a**

[f] **git revert** is a completely different command, used to alter changesets that have already been committed.

[g] N/A

[h] Unsupported

[i] **git fetch** implements the behavior I describe as **pull**; **git pull** is equivalent to **pull** followed by **update**.

9 About Veracity

As of mid-2011, Veracity is a new entry in the DVCS world while Git and Mercurial are already very popular. Some folks wonder how Veracity is different from these other fine tools, so this chapter offers a list of differences. Not everything here should be considered an area where Veracity is better, at least not for all situations. I'm just highlighting differences.

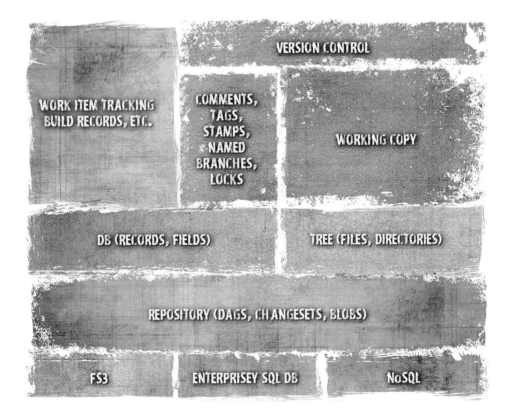

Figure 9.1. Veracity Architecture

1. Decentralized Database

Like any DVCS, Veracity supports versioning of trees, composed of directories and files, with pushing, pulling, and merging of changesets between repository instances.

In addition to trees, Veracity supports the same functionality for *databases*, composed of records and fields, with pushing, pulling, and merging of changesets between repository instances.

Veracity's decentralized database is used for user accounts, audit records, tags, and commit messages. This database is also the platform on which we are building features like bug tracking and build management.

2. User Accounts

Building on its decentralized database, Veracity has support for user accounts, which can be used for administrative functions such as configuring permissions. All repository changes are audited with a timestamp and the userid of the person who made the change.

3. Commercial Open Source

Like Mercurial and Git, Veracity is open source. Unlike Mercurial and Git, Veracity is not a community-driven project.

SourceGear certainly values cooperation at the community level, but Veracity started out very differently from the way Mercurial and Git did.

Both Mercurial and Git were born when the Linux kernel team decided to stop using BitKeeper[1]. They were created primarily to meet the needs of community open source developers.

In contrast, Veracity has (so far) been built entirely by developers employed by SourceGear. It was created primarily to bring the DVCS concept to mainstream corporate development teams.

4. Designed for Integration

Enterprise customers value the ability to customize and integrate the software they use. Regardless of what product they are evaluating, they ask questions about how it can be

---

[1] http://www.bitkeeper.com/

made to work together with all of their other systems. It is not uncommon for these kinds of companies to spend millions of dollars per year to develop and maintain a set of scripts that bridge the gap between the ALM tool they bought and the rest of the systems their company uses.

Veracity was designed to be flexible in this regard.

- It was built as a set of libraries.

- It is written in C, a lowest-common-denominator language that can be ported anywhere.

- It has plugin APIs for repository storage and for push/pull communication with a repository instance.

- It has a scripting engine which allows for a large amount of control and hooks using JavaScript.

- It uses HTTP for push and pull.

- It is fundamentally cross-platform, regularly built and tested on Windows, Mac, and Linux.

5. Apache License 2.0

All three of the most popular and established distributed version control tools (Bazaar, Git, and Mercurial) use the GNU General Public License (GPL). In contrast, Subversion uses the Apache License.

For Veracity, we have chosen to follow Subversion's example in selecting the Apache License 2.0.

The GPL requires that all derived works also be made available under the GPL. This requirement means that GPL-licensed code cannot be used in proprietary software. The Apache License is more permissive about such things.

There is much controversy and debate over these matters. Many companies have concerns about using GPL software, especially in situations where customization and integration work is being done. While the validity of those concerns is in question, the bottom line is very simple: The Apache License is much friendlier to the corporate world than the GPL.

6. Formal Rename and Move

Some version control tools (including Git, for example) implement rename and move **informally**, by deleting the file and adding a new one with the new name or path.

Veracity implements rename and move formally. When a file is created, it gets a unique identifier which never changes and which is distinct from its name or path.[2] Regardless of what happens to that file, its identity stays the same. If and when it gets modified, moved, renamed, or deleted, it is still the same file it was when it was born.

Some people prefer informal rename. They consider it somewhat easier to use.

I, however, am not a fan of informal rename. Some VCS operations, including the merging of branches, need to preserve the identity of a file across a change of its name. To accomplish this, Git has to do some educated guesswork. When Git sees a deleted file in one revision of the tree and an added file in another, it compares the contents of the files to decide if in fact they should be considered the same file. Git's implementation of this guesswork is actually quite clever, usually producing the result the user expects. But not always. I personally prefer a design which allows the user to record exactly what happened, rather than expecting the VCS to divine the user's intentions later. The design of Veracity reflects my preference on this matter.[3]

7. Repository Storage Plugins

As shown in Figure 9.1, Veracity's architecture hides all the details of repository storage behind an API. The 1.0 release of Veracity includes a storage implementation called FS3. By swapping this module for another plugin, it is possible to store a repository instance in another form, such as a SQL database, for example.

The various instances of the same repository can each use their own storage scheme. For example, a team might decide to use FS3 on all the developer desktops while using an enterprise SQL database on a central server.

8. Multiple Working Copies

With Mercurial, Git, and Bazaar, the repository instance usually lives in a hidden directory at the top of the working copy. This means that there is a one-to-one relationship between repository instances and working copies.

---

[2]Eric Raymond refers to this concept as "container identity".
[3]Bazaar supports container identity also.

As mentioned previously, Veracity supports plugins which allow repository data to be stored in a variety of different ways. For this reason, the repository instance is not stored with the working copy.

One nice benefit of this approach is the ability to have multiple working copies for one repository instance.

9. Locks

Veracity's **lock** feature is intended to make Veracity a viable DVCS for teams which manage binary assets under version control.

By its very nature, **lock** cannot be a local-only operation. There is little to be gained by preventing others from modifying a file in your already-private repository instance. So the **lock** operation joins **clone**, **push**, and **pull** as the only core DVCS operations which typically require a network connection.

Veracity allows locking of files only, not directories. Each file lock is held by one user and is limited in scope to a single named branch. In other words, you can't lock a file globally across the whole repository. You can simply say that "file F cannot be modified by anyone else within branch B until my lock is removed".

10. JavaScript

Veracity's scripting language is JavaScript. The core Veracity libraries and executables are all written in C but a JavaScript interpreter[4] is embedded to provide support for several features.

- Veracity exposes a full scripting API to the embedded JavaScript interpreter. We use this API to write our automated test suite and the server side of web applications.
- Hook functions, written in JavaScript, can be registered in a repository to be triggered when certain events happen.
- Veracity uses JSON[5] for all serialized data structures in the repository.
- Veracity includes a framework for writing web applications. The server side of such applications is written in JavaScript using the API mentioned previ-

---

[4]https://developer.mozilla.org/en/SpiderMonkey
[5]http://www.json.org/

ously. Veracity 1.0 includes a web app which supports build tracking, visualization of repository history, bug tracking, an activity stream, and Scrum burn down charts.

11. Stamp

Apply a label which gives information about a given version of the repository.

Veracity introduces a new DVCS operation called Stamp.[6] Stamps can be used to label revisions of the repository with certain attributes. For example, our continuous integration system applies the stamp "goodTests" to each revision of the tree that produced a successful build that also passed the automated test suite.

Veracity's stamps are conceptually similar to Flickr[7] tags, but we couldn't call them "tags" because that word already has a specific meaning in the version control world.

12. Hash Functions

Just like Git and Mercurial, Veracity uses cryptographic hash functions to identify specific revisions. Git and Mercurial use SHA-1. Veracity uses SHA-1 as its default but also supports SHA-2 (at 256, 384, or 512 bits) and Skein (at 256, 512, or 1024 bits).

13. Scrum

In addition to being a DVCS, Veracity has a built-in work item tracking system for agile planning, build management, and tracking bugs. Full coverage of these features is beyond the scope of this book but I'll go ahead and include a couple of pretty pictures.

---

[6]Git's "notes" feature is somewhat similar.
[7]http://www.flickr.com/

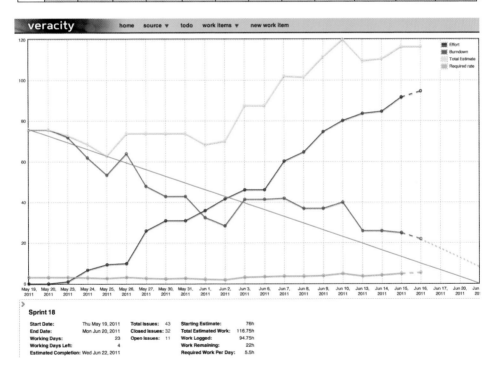

10 Basics with Veracity

Futilisoft has begun work on a new product. This product calculates the probability (as an integer percentage) of winning the Powerball for any given set of numbers.

The company has assigned two developers to work on this new project, Harry, located in Birmingham, England, and Sally, located in Birmingham, Alabama. Both developers are telecommuting to the Futilisoft corporate headquarters in Cleveland. After a bit of discussion, they have decided to implement their product as a command-line app in C and to use Veracity[1] 1.0 for version control.

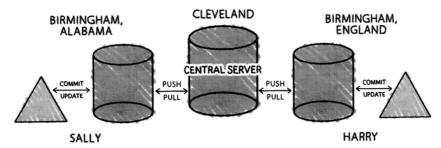

1. Create

Sally gets the project started by creating a new repository.

```
~ server$ mkdir lottery

~ server$ cd lottery

lottery server$ vv init lottery .

lottery server$ vv user create admin
```

---

[1]http://veracity-scm.com/

```
lottery server$ vv whoami admin

lottery server$ vv serve --public
Serving unencrypted on port 8080.
```

I consider the details of server configuration to be too arcane for this book. Let's agree that it happened here and everything went fine.

2. Clone, Add, Status, Commit

By this time Harry is done skiving off and is ready to start coding. First he needs to clone to get his own repository instance.

```
~ harry$ vv clone http://server.futilisoft.com:8080/repos/lottery lottery
Downloading repository...... Done.
Saving new repository... Done.
Use 'vv checkout lottery <path>' to get a working copy.
```

Veracity supports the ability to have more than one working copy per repository instance. It does not store the repository instance in the working copy. Rather, they are stored in an area we call the closet. The location of the closet is configurable. By default it is in
`~/.sgcloset` *(Linux/Mac) or*
`%LOCALAPPDATA%\.sgcloset` *(Windows).*

Now Harry needs a working copy.

```
~ harry$ vv checkout lottery ./lottery

~ harry$ cd lottery
```

Since this is Harry's first time using Veracity, he first sets up his user account.

```
lottery harry$ vv user create harry

lottery harry$ vv whoami harry
```

Harry wonders if Sally has already done anything in the new repository.

```
lottery harry$ ls -al
total 0
drwxr-xr-x   5 harry  staff  170 May 31 10:17 .
drwxr-xr-x  24 harry  staff  816 May 31 10:17 ..
drwxr-xr-x   7 harry  staff  238 May 31 10:17 .sgdrawer
```

Apparently not. Nothing here but the .sgdrawer administrative area. Jolly good then. It's time to start coding. He opens his text editor and creates the starting point for their product.

```c
#include <stdio.h>
#include <stdlib.h>

int calculate_result(int white_balls[5], int power_ball)
{
    return 0;
}

int main(int argc, char** argv)
{
    if (argc != 7)
    {
        fprintf(stderr, "Usage: %s power_ball (5 white balls)\n", argv[0]);
        return -1;
    }

    int power_ball = atoi(argv[1]);

    int white_balls[5];
    for (int i=0; i<5; i++)
    {
        white_balls[i] = atoi(argv[2+i]);
    }

    int result = calculate_result(white_balls, power_ball);

    printf("%d percent chance of winning\n", result);

    return 0;
}
```

Typical of most initial implementations, this is missing a lot of features. But it's a good place to begin. Before committing his code, he wants to make sure it compiles and runs.

```
lottery harry$ gcc -std=c99 lottery.c

lottery harry$ ls -l
total 32
-rwxr-xr-x  1 harry   staff   8904 May 31 10:17 a.out
-rw-r--r--  1 harry   staff    555 May 31 10:17 lottery.c

lottery harry$ ./a.out
Usage: ./a.out power_ball (5 white balls)

lottery harry$ ./a.out 42 1 2 3 4 5
0 percent chance of winning
```

Righto. Time to store this file in the repository. First Harry needs to add the file to the pending changeset.

```
lottery harry$ vv add lottery.c
```

Harry uses the status operation to make sure the pending changeset looks proper.

```
lottery harry$ vv status
   Added:  @/lottery.c
   Found:  @/a.out
```

Veracity is reporting that it found a file it doesn't know what to do about, that a.out file. No time to spit the bit. That's a compiled executable, which should not be stored in a version control repository. He can just ignore that. Now it's time to commit the file.

```
lottery harry$ vv commit -m "initial implementation"

    revision:  2:8d1b667537d569b307e320004ca7cfb10d8aea64
      branch:  master
         who:  harry
        when:  2011/05/31 10:18:23.640 -0500
     comment:  initial implementation
      parent:  1:b669171b03dfcdb78fb332f3d7b09e62d4f05074
```

3. Push, Pull, Log, Diff

Sally now needs to clone to get her own repository instance.

```
~ sally$ vv clone http://server.futilisoft.com:8080/repos/lottery lottery
Downloading repository...... Done.
Saving new repository... Done.
Use 'vv checkout lottery <path>' to get a working copy.
```

Now Sally needs a working copy.

```
~ sally$ vv checkout lottery ./lottery

~ sally$ cd lottery
```

Since this is Sally's first time using Veracity, she first sets up her user account.

```
lottery sally$ vv user create sally

lottery sally$ vv whoami sally
```

OK, let's take a look at the initial code Harry committed.

```
lottery sally$ ls -al
total 0
drwxr-xr-x   3 sally  staff  102 May 31 10:18 .
drwxr-xr-x  25 sally  staff  850 May 31 10:18 ..
drwxr-xr-x   7 sally  staff  238 May 31 10:18 .sgdrawer
```

Hmmm. Harry was supposed to commit the initial code, but there's nothing here.

But Harry did commit his changes! Why aren't they here? Ah, he forgot to push. Sally screams so loud at Harry that he can hear her all the way across the Pond.

```
lottery harry$ vv push
Pushing to http://server.futilisoft.com:8080/repos/lottery:
Pushing... Done.
```

Now Sally can pull.

```
lottery sally$ vv pull
Pulling from http://server.futilisoft.com:8080/repos/lottery:
Pulling... Done.
```

After she has pulled, Sally should have the code, right?

```
lottery sally$ ls -al
total 0
drwxr-xr-x   3 sally  staff  102 May 31 10:18 .
drwxr-xr-x  25 sally  staff  850 May 31 10:18 ..
drwxr-xr-x   7 sally  staff  238 May 31 10:18 .sgdrawer
```

Hmmm. Still not there. Ah, maybe she needs to **vv update** the working copy.

```
lottery sally$ vv update

lottery sally$ ls -al
total 8
drwxr-xr-x   4 sally  staff  136 May 31 10:20 .
drwxr-xr-x  25 sally  staff  850 May 31 10:18 ..
drwxr-xr-x   7 sally  staff  238 May 31 10:20 .sgdrawer
-rw-r--r--   1 sally  staff  555 May 31 10:20 lottery.c
```

Now that she has the initial code they had previously discussed, Sally is happy as a tick on a fat dog. She wants to check the log to see the details.

```
lottery sally$ vv log

    revision:  2:8d1b667537d569b307e320004ca7cfb10d8aea64
      branch:  master
         who:  harry
        when:  2011/05/31 10:18:23.640 -0500
     comment:  initial implementation
      parent:  1:b669171b03dfcdb78fb332f3d7b09e62d4f05074

    revision:  1:b669171b03dfcdb78fb332f3d7b09e62d4f05074
         who:
        when:  2011/05/31 10:16:31.589 -0500
```

> *Note the way Veracity describes this commit: 2:8d1b667537d5.... At the lowest level, a Veracity version ID is a cryptographic hash (SHA-1, by default). This is the part after the colon. Before the colon is a friendlier version number, one which starts at zero and increases by one with each new version. This is more intuitive, but these version numbers are valid only in one repository instance.*

When Sally decides to take a look at the code, she immediately finds something that makes her nervous as a porcupine in a balloon factory. The program expects the red ball number to be the first argument, followed by the other five. But in the actual lottery, the five white numbers are always drawn and shown first. She worries this will be confusing for users so she decides to fix it. Fortunately it is only necessary to modify a few lines of main().

```
    if (argc != 7)
    {
        fprintf(stderr, "Usage: %s (5 white balls) power_ball\n", argv[0]);
        return -1;
    }

    int power_ball = atoi(argv[6]);

    int white_balls[5];
    for (int i=0; i<5; i++)
    {
        white_balls[i] = atoi(argv[1+i]);
    }
```

Now she uses the **status** operation to see the pending changes.

```
lottery sally$ vv status
Modified:  @/lottery.c
```

No surprise there. Veracity knows that lottery.c has been modified. She wants to double-check by reviewing the actual changes.

```
lottery sally$ vv diff
=== ================
===   Modified: File @/lottery.c
--- @/lottery.c 76a16c36b9a4cea4a222ff8132f9f242fa04bed1
+++ @/lottery.c 2011/05/31 15:21:39.000 +0000
@@ -11,16 +11,16 @@
  {
      if (argc != 7)
      {
-         fprintf(stderr, "Usage: %s power_ball (5 white balls)\n", argv[0]);
+         fprintf(stderr, "Usage: %s (5 white balls) power_ball\n", argv[0]);
          return -1;
      }

-     int power_ball = atoi(argv[1]);
+     int power_ball = atoi(argv[6]);

      int white_balls[5];
      for (int i=0; i<5; i++)
      {
```

```
-        white_balls[i] = atoi(argv[2+i]);
+        white_balls[i] = atoi(argv[1+i]);
     }

     int result = calculate_result(white_balls, power_ball);
```

Ain't that the berries!?!

Veracity's diff command can be configured to integrate with any file comparison tool the user prefers. But we also included a special command which gives seamless integration with SourceGear DiffMerge[2], our free application for comparing and merging, supported on Windows, Mac, and Linux.

```
lottery sally$ vv diffmerge
```

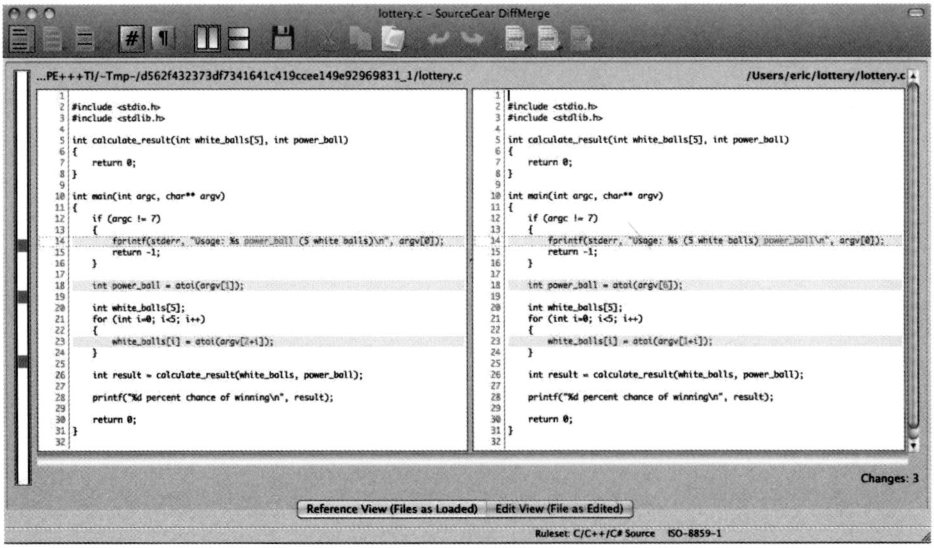

Figure 10.1. Sally's Changes

[2]http://www.sourcegear.com/diffmerge/

4. Update, Commit (with a merge)

Meanwhile, Harry has been coding as well. He heard somebody say that it's best to compile with all the warnings turned on, so he decides to give it a try.

```
lottery harry$ gcc -std=c99 -Wall -Wextra -Werror lottery.c
cc1: warnings being treated as errors
lottery.c:5: warning: unused parameter 'white_balls'
lottery.c:5: warning: unused parameter 'power_ball'
```

I say! The code has some warnings. The `calculate_result()` function isn't using its parameters. Harry looks at the situation and realises the problem immediately: That function should be checking its arguments for validity! The power ball can be from 1 to 39 inclusive. The white balls can be 1 to 59 inclusive. So he implements the error checking.

```c
int calculate_result(int white_balls[5], int power_ball)
{
    for (int i=0; i<5; i++)
    {
        if (
            (white_balls[i] < 1)
            || (white_balls[i] > 59)
            )
        {
            return -1;
        }
    }

    if (
        (power_ball < 1)
        || (power_ball > 39)
        )
    {
        return -1;
    }

    return 0;
}
```

Grand. Let's see if it compiles.

```
lottery harry$ gcc -std=c99 -Wall -Wextra -Werror lottery.c

lottery harry$ ls -l
total 32
-rwxr-xr-x  1 harry  staff  8904 May 31 10:22 a.out
-rw-r--r--  1 harry  staff   843 May 31 10:22 lottery.c
```

Quite. But Harry decides to diff before committing, just for good measure.

```
lottery harry$ vv diff
=== =================
===   Modified: File @/lottery.c
--- @/lottery.c 76a16c36b9a4cea4a222ff8132f9f242fa04bed1
+++ @/lottery.c 2011/05/31 15:22:18.000 +0000
@@ -4,6 +4,25 @@

 int calculate_result(int white_balls[5], int power_ball)
 {
+    for (int i=0; i<5; i++)
+    {
+        if (
+            (white_balls[i] < 1)
+            || (white_balls[i] > 59)
+            )
+        {
+            return -1;
+        }
+    }
+
+    if (
+        (power_ball < 1)
+        || (power_ball > 39)
+        )
+    {
+        return -1;
+    }
+
     return 0;
 }
```

Good show. Time to commit the change.

```
lottery harry$ vv commit -m "fix some warnings"

    revision:  3:7290fd8b3372dfecf5622dec12284d602553258e
      branch:  master
         who:  harry
        when:  2011/05/31 10:23:07.968 -0500
     comment:  fix some warnings
      parent:  2:8d1b667537d569b307e320004ca7cfb10d8aea64
```

No problems there. This time he remembers that he needs to push his changes to the server.

But Sally has been working at the same time and she had her change ready to commit and push first.

```
lottery sally$ vv commit -m "change order of the command line args to be \
                       more like what the user will expect"

   revision:  3:7414ae0aa096674df94e6f3e142e893709ff3ac6
     branch:  master
        who:  sally
       when:  2011/05/31 10:23:57.285 -0500
    comment:  change order of the command line args to be more like
              what the user will expect
     parent:  2:8d1b667537d569b307e320004ca7cfb10d8aea64

lottery sally$ vv push
Pushing to http://server.futilisoft.com:8080/repos/lottery:
Pushing... Done.
```

So Harry tries to push his changes.

```
lottery harry$ vv push
Error:  The push would create new heads in a named branch: master
```

What's all this then? Veracity is not allowing Harry to push his change because it would result in the master branch having two heads.

Harry uses pull to bring in changes.

```
lottery harry$ vv pull
Pulling from http://server.futilisoft.com:8080/repos/lottery:
Pulling... Done.

lottery harry$ vv heads

   revision:  3:7290fd8b3372dfecf5622dec12284d602553258e
     branch:  master
        who:  harry
       when:  2011/05/31 10:23:07.968 -0500
    comment:  fix some warnings
     parent:  2:8d1b667537d569b307e320004ca7cfb10d8aea64

   revision:  4:7414ae0aa096674df94e6f3e142e893709ff3ac6
     branch:  master
        who:  sally
       when:  2011/05/31 10:23:57.285 -0500
    comment:  change order of the command line args to be more like
              what the user will expect
     parent:  2:8d1b667537d569b307e320004ca7cfb10d8aea64

lottery harry$ vv branch list
master (needs merge)
```

Harry can see from the output of **vv heads** that the master branch is now ambiguous and needs to be merged.

```
lottery harry$ vv merge
1 updated, 0 deleted, 0 added, 1 merged, 0 unresolved
```

Splendid. Now the merge is in the working copy.

```
lottery harry$ vv status
Modified:  @/lottery.c
   Found:  @/a.out
```

Everything seems to be ship-shape and Bristol fashion. Harry wants to see what happened.

```
lottery harry$ vv diff
=== =================
===   Modified: File @/lottery.c
--- @/lottery.c 603c9fe57661de7967b3926feb3cf29438dfcbda
+++ @/lottery.c 2011/05/31 15:24:47.000 +0000
@@ -30,16 +30,16 @@
 {
     if (argc != 7)
     {
-        fprintf(stderr, "Usage: %s power_ball (5 white balls)\n", argv[0]);
+        fprintf(stderr, "Usage: %s (5 white balls) power_ball\n", argv[0]);
         return -1;
     }

-    int power_ball = atoi(argv[1]);
+    int power_ball = atoi(argv[6]);

     int white_balls[5];
     for (int i=0; i<5; i++)
     {
-        white_balls[i] = atoi(argv[2+i]);
+        white_balls[i] = atoi(argv[1+i]);
     }

     int result = calculate_result(white_balls, power_ball);
```

Interesting. Diff shows Sally's changes. This is because the diff was performed against changeset 7290fd8b3372dfecf5622dec12284d602553258e. Harry types **vv parents** to see the version of the tree on which his current pending changeset is based.

```
lottery harry$ vv parents

  revision:  3: 7290fd8b3372dfecf5622dec12284d602553258e
    branch:  master
       who:  harry
      when:  2011/05/31 10:23:07.968 -0500
   comment:  fix some warnings
```

```
   parent:  2:8d1b667537d569b307e320004ca7cfb10d8aea64

 revision:  4:7414ae0aa096674df94e6f3e142e893709ff3ac6
   branch:  master
      who:  sally
     when:  2011/05/31 10:23:57.285 -0500
  comment:  change order of the command line args to be more like
            what the user will expect
   parent:  2:8d1b667537d569b307e320004ca7cfb10d8aea64
```

Because it is a merge, his working copy has **two** parents. The resulting DAG node will
have two parents as well.

His code is already committed. Apparently Veracity was able to merge Sally's changes
directly into Harry's modified copy of the file without any conflicts. Smashing! Let's see
if it compiles.

```
lottery harry$ gcc -std=c99 -Wall -Wextra -Werror lottery.c

lottery harry$ ls -l
total 32
-rwxr-xr-x  1 harry  staff  8904 May 31 10:25 a.out
-rw-r--r--  1 harry  staff   843 May 31 10:24 lottery.c
```

Very well then. So Harry is ready to commit the merge.

```
lottery harry$ vv commit -m "merge"

 revision:  5:ee2493eac8e7fc751e2b57a87a3768a192770ae3
   branch:  master
      who:  harry
     when:  2011/05/31 10:25:47.532 -0500
  comment:  merge
  parent :  3:7290fd8b3372dfecf5622dec12284d602553258e
  parent :  4:7414ae0aa096674df94e6f3e142e893709ff3ac6
```

And now **vv parents** shows only one node but that node has two parents.

```
lottery harry$ vv parents
Parents of pending changes in working copy:

 revision:  5:ee2493eac8e7fc751e2b57a87a3768a192770ae3
   branch:  master
      who:  harry
     when:  2011/05/31 10:25:47.532 -0500
  comment:  merge
   parent:  3:7290fd8b3372dfecf5622dec12284d602553258e
   parent:  4:7414ae0aa096674df94e6f3e142e893709ff3ac6
```

And push.

```
lottery harry$ vv push
Pushing to http://server.futilisoft.com:8080/repos/lottery:
Pushing... Done.
```

5. Update (with merge)

Meanwhile, Sally is fixin' to go ahead and add a feature that was requested by the sales team: If the user chooses the lucky number 7 as the red ball, the chances of winning are doubled. Since she is starting a new task, she decides to begin with pull and update to make sure she has the latest code.

```
lottery sally$ vv pull
Pulling from http://server.futilisoft.com:8080/repos/lottery:
Pulling... Done.

lottery sally$ vv update

lottery sally$ vv parents
Parents of pending changes in working copy:

    revision:  5:ee2493eac8e7fc751e2b57a87a3768a192770ae3
      branch:  master
         who:  harry
        when:  2011/05/31 10:25:47.532 -0500
     comment:  merge
      parent:  4:7290fd8b3372dfecf5622dec12284d602553258e
      parent:  3:7414ae0aa096674df94e6f3e142e893709ff3ac6
```

Then she implements the lucky 7 feature in two shakes of a lamb's tail by adding just a few lines of new code to main().

```
lottery sally$ vv diff
=== ================
===   Modified: File @/lottery.c
--- @/lottery.c e3d1f5b0034e4d190e76b993e67d3e2bd24072ed
+++ @/lottery.c 2011/05/31 15:27:06.000 +0000
@@ -44,6 +44,11 @@

     int result = calculate_result(white_balls, power_ball);

+    if (7 == power_ball)
+    {
+        result = result * 2;
+    }
+
     printf("%d percent chance of winning\n", result);

     return 0;
```

And commits her change. And pushes it too.

```
lottery sally$ vv commit -m "lucky 7"

    revision:  6:d494106a9a796e4887aa8de464d825aa76a59a0b
      branch:  master
         who:  sally
        when:  2011/05/31 10:27:31.083 -0500
     comment:  lucky 7
      parent:  5:ee2493eac8e7fc751e2b57a87a3768a192770ae3

lottery sally$ vv push
Pushing to http://server.futilisoft.com:8080/repos/lottery:
Pushing... Done.
```

Meanwhile, Harry has realised his last change had a bug. He modified calculate_result() to return -1 for invalid arguments but he forgot to modify the caller to handle the error. As a consequence, entering a ball number that is out of range causes the program to behave improperly.

```
lottery harry$ ./a.out 61 2 3 4 5 42
-1 percent chance of winning
```

The percent chance of winning certainly can't be a negative number, now can it? So Harry adds an extra check for this case.

```
lottery harry$ vv diff
=== ================
===   Modified: File @/lottery.c
--- @/lottery.c e3d1f5b0034e4d190e76b993e67d3e2bd24072ed
+++ @/lottery.c 2011/05/31 15:28:08.000 +0000
@@ -44,6 +44,12 @@

      int result = calculate_result(white_balls, power_ball);

+     if (result < 0)
+     {
+         fprintf(stderr, "Invalid arguments\n");
+         return -1;
+     }
+
      printf("%d percent chance of winning\n", result);

      return 0;
```

And proceeds to commit and push the fix.

```
lottery harry$ vv commit -m "propagate error code"

    revision:  6:dc13f09452dbc1e24d2ad68b1fba917ef1856b61
      branch:  master
         who:  harry
        when:  2011/05/31 10:28:33.769 -0500
     comment:  propagate error code
      parent:  5:ee2493eac8e7fc751e2b57a87a3768a192770ae3

lottery harry$ vv push
Error: The push would create new heads in a named branch: master
```

Blimey! Sally must have pushed a new changeset already. Harry once again needs to pull and merge to combine Sally's changes with his own.

```
lottery harry$ vv pull
Pulling from http://server.futilisoft.com:8080/repos/lottery:
Pulling... Done.

lottery harry$ vv heads

    revision:  7:d494106a9a796e4887aa8de464d825aa76a59a0b
      branch:  master
         who:  sally
        when:  2011/05/31 10:27:31.083 -0500
     comment:  lucky 7
      parent:  5:ee2493eac8e7fc751e2b57a87a3768a192770ae3

    revision:  6:dc13f09452dbc1e24d2ad68b1fba917ef1856b61
      branch:  master
         who:  harry
        when:  2011/05/31 10:28:33.769 -0500
     comment:  propagate error code
      parent:  5:ee2493eac8e7fc751e2b57a87a3768a192770ae3
```

```
lottery harry$ vv merge
1 updated, 0 deleted, 0 added, 1 merged, 1 unresolved
```

The merge didn't go quite as smoothly this time. Harry wonders if anyone would notice if he were to take the Wumpty down to the pub. Apparently there was a conflict. Harry decides to open up `lottery.c` in his editor to examine the situation.

```
...
    int result = calculate_result(white_balls, power_ball);

<<<<<<< Baseline: BASELINE~lottery.c: /Users/harry/lottery/.sgdrawer/t/merge_2011...
    if (result < 0)
    {
        fprintf(stderr, "Invalid arguments\n");
        return -1;
```

```
    }
=======
    if (7 == power_ball)
    {
        result = result * 2;
    }

>>>>>>> Other: OTHER~lottery.c: /Users/harry/lottery/.sgdrawer/t/merge_2011...
    printf("%d percent chance of winning\n", result);

    return 0;
...
```

Veracity has included both Harry's code and Sally's code with conflict markers to delimit things. What we want is to include both blocks of code. Sally's new code can simply be included right after Harry's error checking.

```
...
    int result = calculate_result(white_balls, power_ball);

    if (result < 0)
    {
        fprintf(stderr, "Invalid arguments\n");
        return -1;
    }

    if (7 == power_ball)
    {
        result = result * 2;
    }

    printf("%d percent chance of winning\n", result);

    return 0;
...
```

That should take care of the problem. Harry compiles the code to make sure and then commits the merge.

```
lottery harry$ vv commit -m "merge"
Error: Cannot commit with unresolved merge issues.
```

Crikey! Now what? Harry fixed the conflict in `lottery.c` but Veracity doesn't seem to know that.

```
lottery harry$ vv resolve list
Unresolved contents conflict on File: @/lottery.c
  Status: Modified
  Baseline Path: @/lottery.c
```

```
Problem: Merge couldn't generate the item's contents.
Cause(s):
   Edit/Edit: Changes to item's contents in different branches conflict.
Possible Contents: (use 'diff' to examine, * indicates merge leaf)
   ancestor
   baseline*
   other*
   merge:     automatically merged from 'baseline' and 'other' with ':merge'
   working*
```

Ah yes. Harry realises that he forgot to tell Veracity that he had resolved the conflict. He uses **resolve** to let Veracity know that the problem has been dealt with.

```
lottery harry$ vv resolve accept working lottery.c
Accepted 'working' value for 'contents' conflict on File:
   @/lottery.c

lottery harry$ vv resolve list
```

There, that looks much better. Harry tries again to commit the merge.

```
lottery harry$ vv commit -m "merge"

    revision:  8:817b33a44fd16f268c6bd0f75b95aaf32e461554
      branch:  master
         who:  harry
        when:  2011/05/31 10:29:50.892 -0500
     comment:  merge
      parent:  7:d494106a9a796e4887aa8de464d825aa76a59a0b
      parent:  6:dc13f09452dbc1e24d2ad68b1fba917ef1856b61
```

And then to retry the push.

```
lottery harry$ vv push
Pushing to http://server.futilisoft.com:8080/repos/lottery:
Pushing... Done.
```

That's put paid to that.

6. Move

Harry immediately moves on to his next task, which is to restructure the tree a bit. He doesn't want the top level of the repository to get too cluttered so he decides to move their vast number of source code files into a src subdirectory.

```
lottery harry$ mkdir src

lottery harry$ vv move lottery.c src

lottery harry$ vv st
    Added:  @/src/
    Moved:  @/src/lottery.c
          # was at @/
    Found:  @/a.out

lottery harry$ vv commit -m "dir structure"

    revision:  9:519ea522ac74f7f1764088d98478f8f569b65f18
      branch:  master
         who:  harry
        when:  2011/05/31 10:30:39.162 -0500
     comment:  dir structure
      parent:  8:817b33a44fd16f268c6bd0f75b95aaf32e461554

lottery harry$ vv push
Pushing to http://server.futilisoft.com:8080/repos/lottery:
Pushing... Done.
```

Sally decides having the number 7 as a constant in the code is ugly enough to stop an eight-day clock. She adds a #define to give it a more meaningful name.

```
lottery sally$ vv diff
=== ================
===   Modified: File @/lottery.c
--- @/lottery.c 5b6f6ebaab98dbfe3386f90436af79dc142482f2
+++ @/lottery.c 2011/05/31 15:31:07.000 +0000
@@ -2,6 +2,8 @@
 #include <stdio.h>
 #include <stdlib.h>

+#define LUCKY_NUMBER 7
+
 int calculate_result(int white_balls[5], int power_ball)
 {
     for (int i=0; i<5; i++)
@@ -50,7 +52,7 @@
        return -1;
    }

-    if (7 == power_ball)
+    if (LUCKY_NUMBER == power_ball)
     {
         result = result * 2;
     }
```

And immediately commits and pushes the change.

```
lottery sally$ vv commit -m "use a #define for the lucky number"

    revision:  9:b5b788895d07b660b2b9213f089383a88d201d27
      branch:  master
         who:  sally
        when:  2011/05/31 10:31:45.918 -0500
     comment:  use a #define for the lucky number
      parent:  8:817b33a44fd16f268c6bd0f75b95aaf32e461554

lottery sally$ vv push
Error: The push would create new heads in a named branch: master
```

Hmmm. Sally needs to pull and merge before she can push her changes.

```
lottery sally$ vv pull
Pulling from http://server.futilisoft.com:8080/repos/lottery:
Pulling... Done.
```

She uses **vv heads** to get a look at the merge situation.

```
lottery sally$ vv heads

    revision:  10:519ea522ac74f7f1764088d98478f8f569b65f18
      branch:  master
         who:  harry
        when:  2011/05/31 10:30:39.162 -0500
     comment:  dir structure
      parent:  8:817b33a44fd16f268c6bd0f75b95aaf32e461554

    revision:  9:b5b788895d07b660b2b9213f089383a88d201d27
      branch:  master
         who:  sally
        when:  2011/05/31 10:31:45.918 -0500
     comment:  use a #define for the lucky number
      parent:  8:817b33a44fd16f268c6bd0f75b95aaf32e461554
```

And proceeds to attempt the merge itself.

```
lottery sally$ vv merge
1 updated, 0 deleted, 1 added, 0 merged, 0 unresolved

lottery sally$ vv st
    Added:  @/src/
    Moved:  @/src/lottery.c
         # was at @/
    Found:  @/a.out
```

No problems on the merge.

```
lottery sally$ vv commit -m "merge"

    revision:  11:3cc62d4c79e2f3a94bb2731e84d2304a10760938
      branch:  master
         who:  sally
        when:  2011/05/31 10:32:44.349 -0500
     comment:  merge
      parent:  10:519ea522ac74f7f1764088d98478f8f569b65f18
      parent:  9:b5b788895d07b660b2b9213f089383a88d201d27

lottery sally$ vv push
Pushing to http://server.futilisoft.com:8080/repos/lottery:
Pushing... Done.
```

7. Rename

Harry decides the time has come to create a proper `Makefile`. And also to gratuitously rename `lottery.c`.

```
lottery harry$ vv add Makefile

lottery harry$ vv rename src/lottery.c pb.c

lottery harry$ vv st
   Added:  @/Makefile
 Renamed:  @/src/pb.c
        # was lottery.c
   Found:  @/a.out
   Found:  @/pb
```

*Note that Veracity has separate commands for **rename** and **move**. Its architecture treats the name of the file as a distinct attribute from the directory in which it resides.*

```
lottery harry$ vv commit -m "Makefile. and lottery.c was too long to type."

    revision:  12:674a480f641b6f206fac2aad1751ae44946a80f6
      branch:  master
         who:  harry
        when:  2011/05/31 10:58:49.906 -0500
     comment:  Makefile. and lottery.c was too long to type.
```

```
    parent:  11:3cc62d4c79e2f3a94bb2731e84d2304a10760938

lottery harry$ vv push
Pushing to http://server.futilisoft.com:8080/repos/lottery:
Pushing... Done.
```

Sally maintains her momentum with #define and adds names for the ball ranges.

```
lottery sally$ vv diff
=== ================
===   Modified: File @/lottery.c
--- @/src/lottery.c 4da6892d436bbab66c980639d3c975cc2da28f99
+++ @/src/lottery.c 2011/05/31 15:59:47.000 +0000
@@ -3,6 +3,8 @@
 #include <stdlib.h>

 #define LUCKY_NUMBER 7
+#define MAX_WHITE_BALL 59
+#define MAX_POWER_BALL 39

 int calculate_result(int white_balls[5], int power_ball)
 {
@@ -10,7 +12,7 @@
     {
         if (
             (white_balls[i] < 1)
-            || (white_balls[i] > 59)
+            || (white_balls[i] > MAX_WHITE_BALL)
           )
         {
             return -1;
@@ -19,7 +21,7 @@

     if (
         (power_ball < 1)
-        || (power_ball > 39)
+        || (power_ball > MAX_POWER_BALL)
       )
     {
       return -1;
```

And commits her changes.

```
lottery sally$ vv commit -m "more #defines"

  revision:  12:d68d482736fecc60549110855becd2e0155f1ef5
    branch:  master
       who:  sally
      when:  2011/05/31 11:00:25.105 -0500
   comment:  more #defines
```

```
      parent:  11:3cc62d4c79e2f3a94bb2731e84d2304a10760938

lottery sally$ vv push
Error: The push would create new heads in a named branch: master
```

Grrr. That Harry is dumber than a coal bucket.

```
lottery sally$ vv pull
Pulling from http://server.futilisoft.com:8080/repos/lottery:
Pulling... Done.

lottery sally$ vv heads

    revision:  13:674a480f641b6f206fac2aad1751ae44946a80f6
      branch:  master
         who:  harry
        when:  2011/05/31 10:58:49.906 -0500
     comment:  Makefile. and lottery.c was too long to type.
      parent:  11:3cc62d4c79e2f3a94bb2731e84d2304a10760938

    revision:  12:d68d482736fecc60549110855becd2e0155f1ef5
      branch:  master
         who:  sally
        when:  2011/05/31 11:00:25.105 -0500
     comment:  more #defines
      parent:  11:3cc62d4c79e2f3a94bb2731e84d2304a10760938

lottery sally$ vv merge
1 updated, 0 deleted, 1 added, 0 merged, 0 unresolved

lottery sally$ make
gcc -std=c99 -Wall -Wextra -Werror src/pb.c -o pb

lottery sally$ vv commit -m "merge"

    revision:  14:b11eaca1a7be8684069e9ce461f42f834acae344
      branch:  master
         who:  sally
        when:  2011/05/31 11:01:19.139 -0500
     comment:  merge
      parent:  13:674a480f641b6f206fac2aad1751ae44946a80f6
      parent:  12:d68d482736fecc60549110855becd2e0155f1ef5

lottery sally$ vv push
Pushing to http://server.futilisoft.com:8080/repos/lottery:
Pushing... Done.
```

8. Delete

Harry wants to get a head start on Zawinski's Law, so he decides to add an IMAP protocol library to their tree.

```
lottery harry$ vv add libvmime-0.9.1

lottery harry$ vv commit -m "add libvmime so we can do the mail reader feature"

    revision:  15:5500274b7b84a5564929a0fb294d553f4a553008
      branch:  master
         who:  harry
        when:  2011/05/31 11:04:59.204 -0500
     comment:  add libvmime so we can do the mail reader feature
      parent:  14:b11eaca1a7be8684069e9ce461f42f834acae344

lottery harry$ vv push
Pushing to http://server.futilisoft.com:8080/repos/lottery:
Pushing... Done.
```

Sally does a pull and finds something that makes her mad as a mule chewing on bumblebees.

```
lottery sally$ vv pull
Pulling from http://server.futilisoft.com:8080/repos/lottery:
Pulling... Done.

lottery sally$ vv update

lottery sally$ ls -l
total 32
-rw-r--r--   1 sally  staff    66 May 31 11:01 Makefile
drwxr-xr-x  29 sally  staff   986 May 31 11:05 libvmime-0.9.1
-rwxr-xr-x   1 sally  staff  8952 May 31 11:01 pb
drwxr-xr-x   3 sally  staff   102 May 31 11:01 src
```

Sally remembers that the specification says the product isn't supposed to include a full email reader until the next release. For the entire 1.0 development cycle, that third party library is going to be about as useful as a snooze button on a fire alarm. So she deletes it.

```
lottery sally$ vv rm libvmime-0.9.1

lottery sally$ vv commit -m "no mail reader until 2.0"

    revision:  16:7590c00819c05cd2103b29216350377c0746ae13
      branch:  master
         who:  sally
        when:  2011/05/31 11:06:37.293 -0500
     comment:  no mail reader until 2.0
      parent:  15:5500274b7b84a5564929a0fb294d553f4a553008
```

```
lottery sally$ vv push
Pushing to http://server.futilisoft.com:8080/repos/lottery:
Pushing... Done.
```

9. Lock, Revert

Fed up with conflicts, Sally decides to lock pb.c so only she can modify it.

> *The decentralized architecture required us to make certain compromises in the implementation of this feature. Obtaining a lock requires a live network connection to wherever you normally push. It is also possible to create local changesets which violate a lock about which you are not yet aware, which will result in a lock violation error later when you attempt to push those changes.*

```
lottery sally$ vv lock src/pb.c
Pulling... Done.
Pushing... Done.
```

Harry updates his repository instance.

```
lottery harry$ vv pull
Pulling from http://server.futilisoft.com:8080/repos/lottery:
Pulling... Done.

lottery harry$ vv update

lottery harry$ ls -l
total 32
-rw-r--r--  1 harry  staff    66 May 31 10:58 Makefile
-rwxr-xr-x  1 harry  staff  8952 May 31 10:58 pb
drwxr-xr-x  3 harry  staff   102 May 31 10:58 src
```

Pants! That Sally must be in a nark. She's deleted all his email code! Harry decides to indent[3] pb.c.

```
lottery harry$ indent src/pb.c

lottery sally$ vv commit -m "indent our code"
Error: @/src/pb.c is locked by sally
```

Such a mithering. Harry calms down and reverts the changes.

> *In this case, the commit failed with a lock violation because Harry did a pull after Sally grabbed the lock. If he had not, the commit would have succeeded, but a subsequent attempt to push would have failed.*

```
lottery harry$ vv revert src/pb.c

lottery harry$ vv st
   Found:  @/pb
   Found:  @/pb.c.BAK

lottery harry$ rm src/pb.c.BAK
```

Sally, basking in the comfort of her lock, makes her edits. She has decided to eliminate uses of atoi(), which is deprecated.

```
lottery sally$ vv diff
=== ================
===   Modified: File @/src/pb.c
--- @/src/pb.c  eb093372fc2d0461465c2fbc0fef5dea54c4c898
+++ @/src/pb.c  2011/05/31 16:27:06.000 +0000
@@ -43,7 +43,14 @@
     int white_balls[5];
     for (int i=0; i<5; i++)
     {
-        white_balls[i] = atoi(argv[1+i]);
+        char* endptr = NULL;
+        long val = strtol(argv[1+i], &endptr, 10);
+        if (*endptr)
+        {
+            fprintf(stderr, "Invalid arguments\n");
```

---

[3]http://en.wikipedia.org/wiki/Indent_(Unix)

```
+            return -1;
+        }
+        white_balls[i] = (int) val;
    }

    int result = calculate_result(white_balls, power_ball);

lottery sally$ make
gcc -std=c99 -Wall -Wextra -Werror pb.c -o pb

lottery sally$ ./pb 1 2 3 4 5 6
0 percent chance of winning

lottery sally$ ./pb 1 2 3e 4 5 6
Invalid arguments
```

And she commits her changes, lickety split.

```
lottery sally$ vv commit -m "use strtol. atoi is deprecated."

    revision:  17:d934a35fc8eda4fec7cb6b0d049e3881cd0e4a1d
      branch:  master
         who:  sally
        when:  2011/05/31 11:28:05.327 -0500
     comment:  use strtol. atoi is deprecated.
      parent:  16:7590c00819c05cd2103b29216350377c0746ae13

lottery sally$ vv push
Pushing to http://server.futilisoft.com:8080/repos/lottery:
Pushing... Done.
```

Veracity does not automatically remove a lock upon commit. Locks must be explicitly removed.

```
lottery sally$ vv unlock src/pb.c
```

10. Tag

Still mourning the loss of his email code, Harry creates a tag so he can more easily access it later.

```
lottery harry$ vv log
...
    revision:  15:5500274b7b84a5564929a0fb294d553f4a553008
         who:  harry
        when:  2011/05/31 11:04:59.204 -0500
     comment:  add libvmime so we can do the mail reader feature
      parent:  14:b11eaca1a7be8684069e9ce461f42f834acae344
...
lottery harry$ vv tag add -r 15 \
    just_before_sally_deleted_my_email_code
```

Harry used the revision number (15) here. Alternatively, he could have specified the changeset ID (5500274b7b84...).

```
lottery harry$ vv log
    revision:  16:7590c00819c05cd2103b29216350377c0746ae13
      branch:  master
         who:  sally
        when:  2011/05/31 11:06:37.293 -0500
     comment:  no mail reader until 2.0
      parent:  15:5500274b7b84a5564929a0fb294d553f4a553008

    revision:  15:5500274b7b84a5564929a0fb294d553f4a553008
         who:  harry
        when:  2011/05/31 11:04:59.204 -0500
         tag:  just_before_sally_deleted_my_email_code
     comment:  add libvmime so we can do the mail reader feature
      parent:  14:b11eaca1a7be8684069e9ce461f42f834acae344
...
```

Veracity stores tags using its decentralized database. Adding a tag does not alter the version control DAG.

```
lottery harry$ vv push
Pushing to http://server.futilisoft.com:8080/repos/lottery:
Pushing... Done.
```

Sally sees Harry gloating in the company chat room about his beloved tag, so she does an update.

```
lottery sally$ vv pull
Pulling from http://server.futilisoft.com:8080/repos/lottery:
Pulling... Done.

lottery sally$ vv update

lottery sally$ vv log
...
        revision:  15:5500274b7b84a5564929a0fb294d553f4a553008
            who:  harry
            when:  2011/05/31 11:04:59.204 -0500
            tag:   just_before_sally_deleted_my_email_code
        comment:  add libvmime so we can do the mail reader feature
         parent:  14:b11eaca1a7be8684069e9ce461f42f834acae344
...
```

Sally sees Harry's tag and rolls her eyes. Fine. Whatever.

11. Branch

Sally wants more privacy. She decides to create her own named branch.

```
lottery sally$ vv branch new no_boys_allowed
Working copy attached to no_boys_allowed.
A new head will be created with the next commit.
```

Now that Sally is working in her own branch, she feels much more productive. She adds support for the "favorite" option. When a user is playing his favorite numbers, his chances of winning should be doubled. In doing this, she had to rework the way command-line args are parsed. And she removes an atoi() call she missed last time. And she restructures all the error checking into one place.

So main() now looks like this:

```c
int main(int argc, char** argv)
{
    int balls[6];
    int count_balls = 0;
    int favorite = 0;

    for (int i=1; i<argc; i++)
    {
        const char* arg = argv[i];

        if ('-' == arg[0])
        {
            if (0 == strcmp(arg, "-favorite"))
            {
                favorite = 1;
            }
            else
            {
                goto usage_error;
            }
        }
        else
        {
            char* endptr = NULL;
            long val = strtol(arg, &endptr, 10);
            if (*endptr)
            {
                goto usage_error;
            }
            balls[count_balls++] = (int) val;
        }
    }

    if (6 != count_balls)
    {
        goto usage_error;
    }

    int power_ball = balls[5];

    int result = calculate_result(balls, power_ball);

    if (result < 0)
    {
        goto usage_error;
    }

    if (LUCKY_NUMBER == power_ball)
    {
        result = result * 2;
    }
```

```
    if (favorite)
    {
        result = result * 2;
    }

    printf("%d percent chance of winning\n", result);

    return 0;

usage_error:
    fprintf(stderr, "Usage: %s [-favorite] (5 white balls) power_ball\n", argv[0]);
    return -1;
}
```

*I **despise** if statements without braces. Reviewers of the early drafts of this book observed that I could save 14 lines and fit the previous code listing on a single page if I compromised my principles. I refused.*

She commits her changes, knowing that the commit will succeed because she is working in her private branch.

```
lottery sally$ vv commit -m "add -favorite and cleanup some other stuff"

    revision:  18:37939b07309af8232c44048ca0a1633c982b7506
      branch:  no_boys_allowed
         who:  sally
        when:  2011/05/31 11:41:37.432 -0500
     comment:  add -favorite and cleanup some other stuff
      parent:  17:d934a35fc8eda4fec7cb6b0d049e3881cd0e4a1d

lottery sally$ vv push
Pushing to http://server.futilisoft.com:8080/repos/lottery:
Pushing... Done.
```

12. Merge (no conflicts)

Meanwhile, over in the master branch, Harry decides the white balls should be sorted before analysing them, because that's how they get shown on the idiot's lantern.

```
lottery harry$ vv diff
=== =================
===   Modified: File @/src/pb.c
--- @/src/pb.c  5649f2644a495ba4bf4d2a23d9a28e5c30064cd5
+++ @/src/pb.c  2011/05/31 16:44:53.000 +0000
@@ -6,6 +6,25 @@
 #define MAX_WHITE_BALL 59
 #define MAX_POWER_BALL 39

+static int my_sort_func(const void* p1, const void* p2)
+{
+    int v1 = *((int *) p1);
+    int v2 = *((int *) p2);
+
+    if (v1 < v2)
+    {
+        return -1;
+    }
+    else if (v1 > v2)
+    {
+        return 1;
+    }
+    else
+    {
+        return 0;
+    }
+}
+
 int calculate_result(int white_balls[5], int power_ball)
 {
     for (int i=0; i<5; i++)
@@ -27,6 +46,8 @@
         return -1;
     }

+    qsort(white_balls, 5, sizeof(int), my_sort_func);
+
     return 0;
 }
```

And he commits the change.

```
lottery harry$ vv commit -m "sort the white balls"

    revision:  19:e1ff5a3d4def8a5b45179f5326f68367b2f270c9
      branch:  master
         who:  harry
        when:  2011/05/31 11:46:01.784 -0500
     comment:  sort the white balls
      parent:  17:d934a35fc8eda4fec7cb6b0d049e3881cd0e4a1d
```

But now he's curious about what Sally has been doing. She said he wasn't allowed to commit to her branch but she didn't say anything about **looking** at it.

```
lottery harry$ vv heads

    revision:  18:37939b07309af8232c44048ca0a1633c982b7506
      branch:  no_boys_allowed
         who:  sally
        when:  2011/05/31 11:41:37.432 -0500
     comment:  add -favorite and cleanup some other stuff
      parent:  17:d934a35fc8eda4fec7cb6b0d049e3881cd0e4a1d

    revision:  19:e1ff5a3d4def8a5b45179f5326f68367b2f270c9
      branch:  master
         who:  harry
        when:  2011/05/31 11:46:01.784 -0500
     comment:  sort the white balls
      parent:  17:d934a35fc8eda4fec7cb6b0d049e3881cd0e4a1d
...
```

Interesting. She added the "favorite" feature. Harry decides he wants that. So he asks Veracity to merge stuff from Sally's branch into master.

```
lottery harry$ vv merge -r 37939b07309af8232c44048ca0a1633c982b7506
1 updated, 0 deleted, 0 added, 1 merged, 0 unresolved
```

Harry used **-r 37939b07309a...** *here. He could also have used* **-r 18** *(the local revision number) or* **-b no_boys_allowed** *(the head of Sally's branch).*

Top Ho! Harry examines pb.c and discovers that it was merged correctly. Sally's "favorite" changes are there and his qsort changes are as well. So he compiles the code, runs a quick test, and commits the merge.

```
lottery harry$ make
gcc -std=c99 -Wall -Wextra -Werror pb.c -o pb

lottery harry$ ./pb -favorite 5 3 33 22 7 31
0 percent chance of winning

lottery harry$ vv commit -m "merge changes from sally"

    revision:  20:68f12175bcda2296298f6b0f30da326341976356
```

```
   branch:  master
      who:  harry
     when:  2011/05/31 11:49:49.565 -0500
  comment:  merge changes from sally
   parent:  18:37939b07309af8232c44048ca0a1633c982b7506
   parent:  19:e1ff5a3d4def8a5b45179f5326f68367b2f270c9

lottery harry$ vv push
Pushing to http://server.futilisoft.com:8080/repos/lottery:
Pushing... Done.
```

13. Merge (repeated, no conflicts)

Simultaneously, both Harry and Sally have a crisis of conscience and realize that their code has no comments at all.

Harry:

```
lottery harry$ vv diff
=== ================
===   Modified: File @/src/pb.c
--- @/src/pb.c  3cdd8958d3467042fd5791f3c16951f3cfdacc5c
+++ @/src/pb.c  2011/05/31 16:53:00.000 +0000
@@ -47,6 +47,7 @@
          return -1;
      }

+     // lottery ball numbers are always shown sorted
      qsort(white_balls, 5, sizeof(int), my_sort_func);

      return 0;

lottery harry$ vv commit -m "comments"

   revision:  21:cb3675aada7836e63ec88fc5a6eeb9f80a00f656
     branch:  master
        who:  harry
       when:  2011/05/31 11:53:32.590 -0500
    comment:  comments
     parent:  20:68f12175bcda2296298f6b0f30da326341976356

lottery harry$ vv push
Pushing to http://server.futilisoft.com:8080/repos/lottery:
Pushing... Done.
```

And Sally:

```
lottery sally$ vv diff
=== ================
===   Modified: File @/src/pb.c
--- @/src/pb.c  7d927466a22e24d4adc5542f6bf0a4797aa06801
+++ @/src/pb.c  2011/05/31 16:54:57.000 +0000
@@ -35,7 +35,7 @@
 {
     int balls[6];
     int count_balls = 0;
-    int favorite = 0;
+    int favorite = 0;  // this should be a bool

     for (int i=1; i<argc; i++)
     {
@@ -69,10 +69,13 @@
         goto usage_error;
     }

+    // the power ball is always the last one given
     int power_ball = balls[5];

     int result = calculate_result(balls, power_ball);

+    // calculate result can return -1 if the ball numbers
+    // are out of range
     if (result < 0)
     {
         goto usage_error;

lottery sally$ vv commit -m "comments"

    revision:  21:69f50e32759eef176403ca0c019fb1af73145fb9
      branch:  no_boys_allowed
         who:  sally
        when:  2011/05/31 11:55:40.174 -0500
     comment:  comments
      parent:  18:37939b07309af8232c44048ca0a1633c982b7506

lottery sally$ vv push
Pushing to http://server.futilisoft.com:8080/repos/lottery:
Pushing... Done.
```

Harry decides to try again to merge the changes from Sally's branch.

```
lottery harry$ vv heads

    revision:  22:69f50e32759eef176403ca0c019fb1af73145fb9
      branch:  no_boys_allowed
         who:  sally
        when:  2011/05/31 11:55:40.174 -0500
     comment:  comments
      parent:  18:37939b07309af8232c44048ca0a1633c982b7506
```

```
    revision:  21:cb3675aada7836e63ec88fc5a6eeb9f80a00f656
      branch:  master
         who:  harry
        when:  2011/05/31 11:53:32.590 -0500
     comment:  comments
      parent:  20:68f12175bcda2296298f6b0f30da326341976356

lottery harry$ vv merge -r 69f50e32759eef176403ca0c019fb1af73145fb9
1 updated, 0 deleted, 0 added, 1 merged, 0 unresolved
```

No problems with the merge. Let's review the changes.

```
lottery harry$ vv diff
=== ================
===   Modified: File @/src/pb.c
--- @/src/pb.c  ec840f5b96e6f64ab9efaf0b37975ceafa6bfe81
+++ @/src/pb.c  2011/05/31 16:57:07.000 +0000
@@ -57,7 +57,7 @@
 {
     int balls[6];
     int count_balls = 0;
-    int favorite = 0;
+    int favorite = 0;  // this should be a bool

     for (int i=1; i<argc; i++)
     {
@@ -91,10 +91,13 @@
         goto usage_error;
     }

+    // the power ball is always the last one given
    int power_ball = balls[5];

    int result = calculate_result(balls, power_ball);

+    // calculate result can return -1 if the ball numbers
+    // are out of range
    if (result < 0)
    {
        goto usage_error;
```

Harry checks to see if everything compiles, and commits the merge.

```
lottery harry$ make
gcc -std=c99 -Wall -Wextra -Werror pb.c -o pb

lottery harry$ vv commit -m "merge changes from sally"

    revision:  23:31d8497141637a90feeb38f16ac9ff9454673e3d
      branch:  master
         who:  harry
        when:  2011/05/31 11:57:55.503 -0500
     comment:  merge changes from sally
```

```
    parent:  22:69f50e32759eef176403ca0c019fb1af73145fb9
    parent:  21:cb3675aada7836e63ec88fc5a6eeb9f80a00f656

lottery harry$ vv push
Pushing to http://server.futilisoft.com:8080/repos/lottery:
Pushing... Done.
```

14. Merge (conflicts)

Sally realizes that C99 has a bool type that should have been used.

```
lottery sally$ vv diff
=== ================
===   Modified: File @/src/pb.c
--- @/src/pb.c  a35acfb35567f64a2e20ef246ae44aef89a904bd
+++ @/src/pb.c  2011/05/31 16:59:35.000 +0000
@@ -2,6 +2,7 @@
 #include <stdio.h>
 #include <stdlib.h>
 #include <string.h>
+#include <stdbool.h>

 #define LUCKY_NUMBER 7
 #define MAX_WHITE_BALL 59
@@ -35,7 +36,7 @@
 {
     int balls[6];
     int count_balls = 0;
-    int favorite = 0;  // this should be a bool
+    bool favorite = false;

     for (int i=1; i<argc; i++)
     {
@@ -45,7 +46,7 @@
         {
             if (0 == strcmp(arg, "-favorite"))
             {
-                favorite = 1;
+                favorite = true;
             }
             else
             {
```

And she commits the change to her private branch.

```
lottery sally$ vv commit -m "use the bool type"

    revision:  24:1bb6c0d46c06d7575f39ca82210e586ff56a0ad4
      branch:  no_boys_allowed
         who:  sally
```

```
       when:   2011/05/31 12:00:28.819 -0500
    comment:   use the bool type
     parent:   21:69f50e32759eef176403ca0c019fb1af73145fb9

lottery sally$ vv push
Pushing to http://server.futilisoft.com:8080/repos/lottery:
Pushing... Done.
```

Meanwhile, Harry has been grumbling about Sally's butchering of the Queen's English and decides to correct the spelling of the word "favourite".

```
lottery harry$ vv diff
=== ================
===   Modified: File @/src/pb.c
--- @/src/pb.c  cde51a1d39996efe6e24608d908d9ae9ec93c869
+++ @/src/pb.c  2011/05/31 17:01:23.000 +0000
@@ -57,7 +57,7 @@
 {
     int balls[6];
     int count_balls = 0;
-    int favorite = 0;   // this should be a bool
+    int favourite = 0;   // this should be a bool

     for (int i=1; i<argc; i++)
     {
@@ -65,9 +65,9 @@

         if ('-' == arg[0])
         {
-            if (0 == strcmp(arg, "-favorite"))
+            if (0 == strcmp(arg, "-favourite"))
             {
-                favorite = 1;
+                favourite = 1;
             }
             else
             {
@@ -108,7 +108,7 @@
         result = result * 2;
     }

-    if (favorite)
+    if (favourite)
     {
         result = result * 2;
     }
@@ -118,7 +118,7 @@
     return 0;

 usage_error:
```

```
-      fprintf(stderr, "Usage: %s [-favorite] (5 white balls) power_ball\n", argv[0]);
+      fprintf(stderr, "Usage: %s [-favourite] (5 white balls) power_ball\n", argv[0]);
       return -1;
 }
```

Feeling quite chuffed about his pedantry, Harry proceeds to commit the change.

```
lottery harry$ vv commit -m "fixed spelling error"

    revision:  24:54bc95bef02726d647ce3f3f741048b852c22bef
      branch:  master
         who:  harry
        when:  2011/05/31 12:02:12.841 -0500
     comment:  fixed spelling error
      parent:  23:31d8497141637a90feeb38f16ac9ff9454673e3d
```

```
lottery harry$ vv pull
Pulling from http://server.futilisoft.com:8080/repos/lottery:
Pulling... Done.

lottery harry$ vv heads

    revision:  25:1bb6c0d46c06d7575f39ca82210e586ff56a0ad4
      branch:  no_boys_allowed
         who:  sally
        when:  2011/05/31 12:00:28.819 -0500
     comment:  use the bool type
      parent:  22:69f50e32759eef176403ca0c019fb1af73145fb9

    revision:  24:54bc95bef02726d647ce3f3f741048b852c22bef
      branch:  master
         who:  harry
        when:  2011/05/31 12:02:12.841 -0500
     comment:  fixed spelling error
      parent:  23:31d8497141637a90feeb38f16ac9ff9454673e3d
```

And to once again merge Sally's changes into master.

```
lottery harry$ vv merge -b no_boys_allowed
1 updated, 0 deleted, 0 added, 1 merged, 1 unresolved

lottery harry$ vv st
Modified:  @/src/pb.c
   Found:  @/pb
Conflict:  @/src/pb.c
        # content conflict

# Use the 'vv resolve' command to view more details
# about your conflicts or to resolve them.

lottery harry$ vv resolve list
```

```
Unresolved contents conflict  on File: @/src/pb.c
  Status: Modified
  Baseline Path: @/src/pb.c
  Problem: Merge couldn't generate the item's contents.
  Cause(s):
    Edit/Edit: Changes to item's contents in different branches conflict.
  Possible Contents: (use 'diff' to examine, * indicates merge leaf)
    ancestor
    baseline*
    other*
    merge:      automatically merged from 'baseline' and 'other' with ':merge'
    working
```

Crikey! Conflicts in pb.c again.

```
lottery harry$ vv diff
=== ================
===   Modified: File @/src/pb.c
--- @/src/pb.c   4a36fdc1601f2b9b586b9239f0dd3c928722a00c
+++ @/src/pb.c   2011/05/31 17:03:17.000 +0000
@@ -2,6 +2,7 @@
 #include <stdio.h>
 #include <stdlib.h>
 #include <string.h>
+#include <stdbool.h>

 #define LUCKY_NUMBER 7
 #define MAX_WHITE_BALL 59
@@ -57,7 +58,11 @@
 {
     int balls[6];
     int count_balls = 0;
+<<<<<<< Baseline: BASELINE~pb.c: /Users/harry/lottery/.sgdrawer/t/merge_20110531_0/pb.c...
     int favourite = 0;  // this should be a bool
+=======
+    bool favorite = false;
+>>>>>>> Other: OTHER~pb.c: /Users/harry/lottery/.sgdrawer/t/merge_20110531_0/pb.c...

     for (int i=1; i<argc; i++)
     {
@@ -67,7 +72,11 @@
         {
             if (0 == strcmp(arg, "-favourite"))
             {
+<<<<<<< Baseline: BASELINE~pb.c: /Users/harry/lottery/.sgdrawer/t/merge_20110531_0/pb.c...
                 favourite = 1;
+=======
+                favorite = true;
+>>>>>>> Other: OTHER~pb.c: /Users/harry/lottery/.sgdrawer/t/merge_20110531_0/pb.c...
             }
             else
             {
```

Now that needs a bit of guntering. Harry quickly realises this conflict needs to be resolved manually by keeping the proper spelling but converting the type to bool like Sally did.

```
lottery harry$ vv diff
=== =================
===   Modified: File @/src/pb.c
--- @/src/pb.c  4a36fdc1601f2b9b586b9239f0dd3c928722a00c
+++ @/src/pb.c  2011/05/31 17:06:24.000 +0000
@@ -2,6 +2,7 @@
 #include <stdio.h>
 #include <stdlib.h>
 #include <string.h>
+#include <stdbool.h>

 #define LUCKY_NUMBER 7
 #define MAX_WHITE_BALL 59
@@ -57,7 +58,7 @@
 {
     int balls[6];
     int count_balls = 0;
-    int favourite = 0;  // this should be a bool
+    bool favourite = false;

     for (int i=1; i<argc; i++)
     {
@@ -67,7 +68,7 @@
         {
             if (0 == strcmp(arg, "-favourite"))
             {
-                favourite = 1;
+                favourite = true;
             }
             else
             {
```

After manually merging the changes, Harry proceeds to resolve the conflict and commit the merge.

```
lottery harry$ vv resolve accept working src/pb.c
Accepted 'working' value for 'contents' conflict on File:
   @/src/pb.c

lottery harry$ vv commit -m "merge, conflicts fixed"

    revision:  26:96f8aed89a5d16970c7d4e87b6a96e7d481ed3e9
      branch:  master
         who:  harry
        when:  2011/05/31 12:07:29.931 -0500
     comment:  merge, conflicts fixed
      parent:  25:1bb6c0d46c06d7575f39ca82210e586ff56a0ad4
      parent:  24:54bc95bef02726d647ce3f3f741048b852c22bef
```

```
lottery harry$ vv push
Pushing to http://server.futilisoft.com:8080/repos/lottery:
Pushing... Done.
```

And all of Futilisoft's customers lived happily ever after.

15. Summary

The following screen shot from the Veracity web UI shows the resulting DAG from the 26 changesets just completed by Harry and Sally.

history		comment	date	author
26:96f8aed89a ...	master	merge, conflicts fixed	May 31 at 12:07 harry
25:1bb6c0d46c ...	no_boys_allowed	use the bool type	May 31 at 12:00 sally
24:54bc95bef0 ...		fixed spelling error	May 31 at 12:02 harry
23:31d8497141 ...		merge changes from sally	May 31 at 11:57 harry
22:69f50e3275 ...		comments	May 31 at 11:55 sally
21:cb3675aada ...		comments	May 31 at 11:53 harry
20:68f12175bc ...		merge changes from sally	May 31 at 11:49 harry
19:e1ff5a3d4d ...		sort the white balls	May 31 at 11:46 sally
18:37939b0730 ...		add -favorite and cleanup some other stuff	May 31 at 11:41 sally
17:d934a35fc8 ...		use strtol. atoi is deprecated.	May 31 at 11:28 sally
16:7590c00819 ...		no mail reader until 2.0	May 31 at 11:06 sally
15:5500274b7b ...		add libvmime so we can do the mail reader feature just_before_sally_deleted_my_email_code	May 31 at 11:04 harry
14:b11eaca1a7 ...		merge	May 31 at 11:01 sally
13:d68d482736 ...		more #defines	May 31 at 11:00 sally
12:674a480f64 ...		Makefile. and lottery.c was too long to type.	May 31 at 10:58 harry
11:3cc62d4c79 ...		merge	May 31 at 10:32 sally
10:b5b788895d ...		use a #define for the lucky number	May 31 at 10:31 sally
9:519ea522ac ...		dir structure	May 31 at 10:30 harry
8:817b33a44f ...		merge	May 31 at 10:29 harry
7:d494106a9a ...		lucky 7	May 31 at 10:27 sally
6:dc13f09452 ...		propagate error code	May 31 at 10:28 harry
5:ee2493eac8 ...		merge	May 31 at 10:25 harry
4:7414ae0aa0 ...		change order of the command line args to be more like	May 31 at 10:23 sally
3:7290fd8b33 ...		fix some warnings	May 31 at 10:23 harry
2:8d1b667537 ...		initial implementation	May 31 at 10:18 harry
1:b669171b03 ...			May 31 at 10:16

The following table summarizes all 21 commands for Veracity. See Table A.1 in Appendix A for a comparison of Veracity's commands with other tools.

Operation	Veracity Command
Create	vv init
Checkout	vv checkout
Commit	vv commit
Update	vv update
Add	vv add
Edit	[a]
Delete	vv remove
Rename	vv rename
Move	vv move
Status	vv status
Diff	vv diff
Revert	vv revert
Log	vv log
Tag	vv tag
Branch	vv branch
Merge	vv merge
Resolve	vv resolve
Lock	vv lock[b]
Clone	vv clone
Push	vv push
Pull	vv pull

[a]Automatic: Veracity will notice that the file has changed.

[b]Veracity locks must be explicitly removed.

3

Beyond Basics

11   Workflows

1. Managing Multiple Releases

One of the most important things version control can help you with is the management of multiple releases.

Software teams come in all shapes and sizes, with an enormous variation in the frequency of their releases. Figure 11.1 shows some examples of software teams and a very rough idea of how often they tend to do a release.

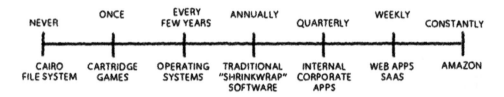

Figure 11.1. Frequency of Releases

The more often you release, the more you need to be using branches to manage things.

2. Shrinkwrap

Let's talk first about traditional shrinkwrap software. This is software which is licensed to be installed on the end user system. The "shrinkwrap" name sounds funny today because most software of this type now gets delivered by download over the Internet with no physical packaging at all. But not that long ago, a lot of software was actually pressed onto CD, placed in a box, and wrapped in cellophane. Many people still use the "shrinkwrap" term for this kind of software even when plastic wrap is not involved.

Even without physical packaging, every release of shrinkwrap software involves a significant amount of overhead for both the developers (updating all the supporting materials and systems) and users (installing everywhere, learning the new features, etc.). Because of this overhead, shrinkwrap software tends to get released every 3-24 months, with annual releases being a typical situation.

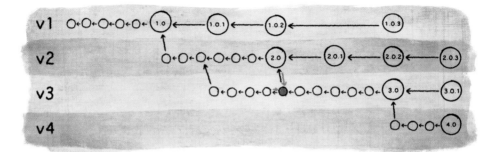

Figure 11.2. Traditional Shrinkwrap

Figure 11.2 illustrates the development of four major releases, along with several maintenance releases. In this development process, the team is working on two or three releases at the same time. Time goes from left to right in the picture.

> *Remember that in my DAG pictures, I always draw the arrows from child to parent. Think of these arrows as meaning "is based on". Nonetheless, for merge nodes, this can feel a bit counterintuitive, since the changesets are flowing in the opposite direction of the arrow. So in this chapter I have shaded the merge nodes green and added an extra green arrow to show how things in the merge operation are moving.*

+ First, after a bunch of work gets done, version 1.0 is released.

+ Version 2.0 development begins immediately, using 1.0 as the starting point.

+ Version 3.0 development begins early, branching off the 2.0 code base before it is complete.

+ To deal with a critical bug-fix, version 1.0.1 is released.

- Version 2.0 is completed and released. Stuff from 2.0 gets merged into the 3.0 branch. For users still on v1, a bug-fix version 1.0.2 is released.
- To deal with a critical bug-fix, version 2.0.1 is released.
- Version 3.0 is completed and released. Bug-fix releases are done for users still on v2 and even on v1. V4 begins with 3.0 as the starting point.
- Version 4.0 is completed and released. Once again, there are bug-fix releases for the two previous versions, resulting in 3.0.1 and 2.0.3, but v1 is too old for continuing the maintenance.

Let's talk specifically about how we can use branches to support this kind of workflow. First, we have our main development branch. We'll call it Master. All of your development work goes here. All new feature work goes in here, and bug-fixes from other branches get merged back into here. Everything finds its way to Master, directly or indirectly. I define my workflows such that Master is usually regarded as "somewhat unstable".[1] Insofar as lots of developers are using it, we want its contents to build and pass test suites. But this is where work-in-progress goes.

2.1. Polishing Branches

As development moves along, at some point it is time to begin preparing for a release. This phase of the cycle is often called "QA" or "Testing", but I prefer not to use terminology which suggests that all testing and bug-fixing is left until the end. Best practices in software development are to find and fix bugs as early as possible. So I call this phase "polishing", which is more suggestive of taking something that is basically done and giving it the detailed attention it needs to have a really fine fit and finish.

The process of polishing your software to make it ready for release is mostly about fixing minor bugs. But sometimes during this phase, stuff happens that should not go into the release.

- Sometimes we identify bug-fixes or improvements that are too risky to be included in the release being polished[2].
- Sometimes feature work on release N+1 begins sometime during the Polishing phase of release N.
- Sometimes, even though we spent some time during the release N cycle building a feature, we decide that feature needs to get postponed until release N+1.

---

[1]Some Git developers use its "master" branch in the manner I describe for a Release branch, treating it as highly stable. This is merely a difference in naming.

[2]http://www.ericsink.com/articles/Four_Questions.html

If none of the above happened, and the Master branch contains **exactly** what will go into the release, and absolutely everything that needs to be committed during the Polishing phase can go into the release currently being Polished, then we don't need a branch.

But that's rare. So we need a branch. We need a way to keep the bug-fixing and polishing of the release separate from everything else.

So we create a new Polishing branch.

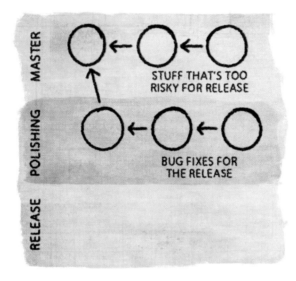

Figure 11.3. A Polishing Branch

- Everybody working on this release should switch and start working in the Polishing branch. All bug-fixes for the release should be committed directly into the Polishing branch, not into the Master branch. They will get merged back into Master later.

- Anything which needs to be committed but does not go into this release should go into Master.

Polishing is a short-lived branch. It exists entirely for the purpose of getting something ready for release. When that something is ready, the Polishing branch is closed.

2.2. Release Branches

When the polishing is done and the software is nice and shiny, it is time for release.

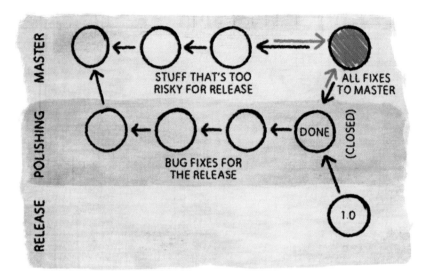

Figure 11.4. A Release Branch

There are three things that happen at Release time.

+ Create a Release branch off the Polishing branch.
+ Merge all the changes from the Polishing branch back into Master.
+ Close the Polishing branch.

You should always have a branch which contains the exact contents of your current release.

Actually, the Release branch almost doesn't need to be a branch. In a perfect world, the release is flawless and this branch will never get any more changes committed to it. A branch which never gets any commits is effectively a tag.

But in reality, critical fixes are sometimes necessary. Users don't always upgrade to the latest release and it is customary to continue providing a certain amount of support and maintenance for older releases, within reason.

+ Sometimes bugs slip through the Polishing phase and an x.0.1 release is necessary.

- Sometimes it is a good idea to do a 1.0.x when 3.0 is released to make their behavior more consistent or compatible in some way.

- Sometimes an x.0.1 release is necessary because some other piece of software changed.

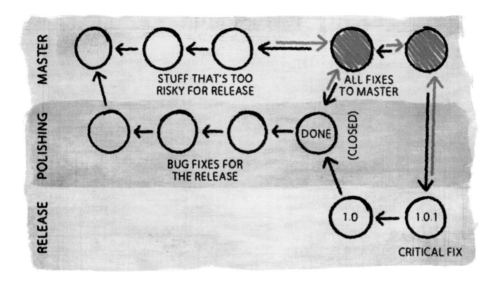

Figure 11.5. Critical Fix

When a critical fix is needed, do the fix in the Release branch. Merge it back to Master.

Note that I have been referring to "the" Release branch, as if there is only one of them. In practice, you should keep an open Release branch for every major version which was released to customers. So your release branches will likely be named something like "Release_v1" and "Release_v2" and so on.

2.3. Feature Branches

Everything I'm saying in this chapter can be considered as a starting point. Your particular situation may be much more complicated. You should feel free to tweak things until you have a workflow that is effective for your team. And make sure you're using a VCS that is flexible enough to adapt with you.

Here's an example:

Sometimes development of new features is too complicated to have just one Master branch. In these situations, it may be helpful to think of Master as a cluster of branches. There is still one main branch called Master where everything eventually ends up, but we also have subordinate branches called "Feature Branches".

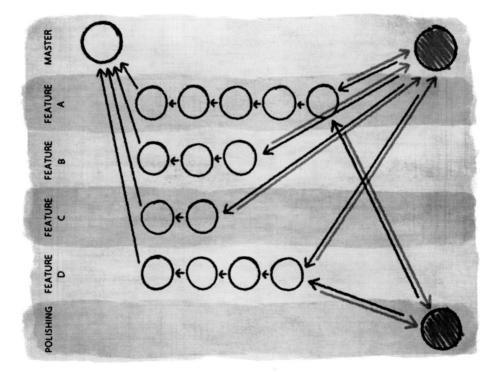

Figure 11.6. Feature Branches

With Feature Branches, developers work on each major feature in a dedicated branch. When the feature is done, it gets merged into Master. But it is also possible to construct a Polishing branch directly from one or more Feature branches. This allows us to make the decision to release only a subset of the features which have been under development.

For example, in Figure 11.6, features B and C are not ready for release, so we construct a Polishing branch which contains only features A and D.

3. Web

With a Web-based application, the notion of a "release" is different, so the way we use the VCS is different.

- For web developers, "release" means deploying new code to the website. That new code immediately becomes available to all users.

- The website has only one version of the software on it. Everybody is always using the latest version. There is no obligation to continue providing support to users who chose to stay with an older version instead of upgrading to the new release.

- Users are generally unaware of versioning. Version numbers are not part of the user's consciousness. People who talk at conferences about their experience with Google Calendar do not ask each other which version they are running.

- For web developers, there isn't much overhead in doing a release, so they can deploy new versions with new features and fixes as often as makes sense. Some major websites deploy changes multiples times per day.

Despite all the differences, there are some ways where the use of a VCS for Web developers is the same. Just as with shrinkwrap, we have a Master branch, the main line of development. Everything finds its way here.

We also have a Release branch, but there's only one of them, and it's a long-lived branch. It always contains the exact code which is currently deployed on the website.

So, omitting the details of Polishing, we can think of a Web app workflow as an ongoing Release branch which periodically merges changes from the ongoing Master branch, as shown in Figure 11.7.

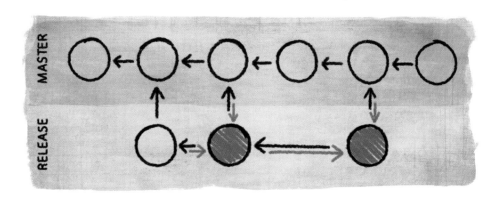

Figure 11.7. Versions of a Web App

We handle critical fixes the same way as well. Do the fix in the Release branch. Merge it back into Master.

Feature branches are perhaps even more important for Web developers than for situations where releases are less frequent. A typical Web app team is a bunch of developers working on a variety of features that are going to be ready for deployment at different times. With a shrinkwrap workflow, we try to get all the features to be done at the same time. If we have a feature that isn't ready for release, we have to (a) slip the release or (b) make the feature miss the boat and wait 12 months until the next departure. With a Web app, each feature can get released whenever it is ready.

When we prepare to do a release, we want to gather the feature(s) that are ready into a Polishing branch so we can integrate and test and polish and make sure they are truly ready for deployment. But if all the features being developed are mixed up together in the same branch, it's a lot harder to grab just the ones we want to deploy. Feature branches make it much easier to pick and choose only certain features, excluding the ones that we need to keep cooking until they're ready.

12 DVCS Internals

Version control tools are more like cars than clocks.

Clock users have no need to know how a clock works behind the dials. We just want to know what time it is. Those who understand the inner workings of a clock can't tell time any more skillfully than the rest of us.

Version control tools are more like cars. Lots of people, including me, use cars without knowing much about how they work. However, people who really understand cars tend to get better performance out of them.

This chapter could be a whole book of its own—I am not giving a comprehensive treatment of how distributed version control tools work. I'll just offer a few highlights that I think are worth knowing:

- I'll use Git to discuss cryptographic hashes.
- I'll use Mercurial to discuss deltified storage.
- I'll use Veracity to discuss DAGs and blob storage. Plus a brief discussion of its decentralized database.

First, let's talk briefly about the concept of a delta.

1. Deltas

One of the first things I said in this book is that a VCS repository contains every version of everything that has ever happened.

So how does the repository store all that stuff? Maybe it just keeps a full snapshot of every version of the tree. Disk space is cheap, right?

Well, it's not **that** cheap. If version control data were stored that way, lots of teams would have repositories of 10 TB or more. Around this point, the common argument that "disk space is cheap" starts to break down. The cost of dealing with 10 TB of important data is much greater than just the cost of the actual disk platters.

Fortunately, there is a huge amount of redundancy in version-controlled data. We observe that tree N is often not terribly different from tree N-1. By definition, each version of the tree is derived from its predecessor. A commit might be as simple as a one-line fix to a single file. All of the other files are unchanged; we don't really need to store another copy of them.

So we don't want to store the full contents of the tree for every single change. Instead, we want a way to store a tree in terms of the changes relative to another tree. We call this a *delta*. All version control tools use some form of delta concept when storing repository data.

A tree is a hierarchy of directories and files. A delta is the difference between two trees. In theory, those two trees do not need to be related. However, in practice, the only reason we calculate the difference between them is because one of them is derived from the other. Some developer started with tree N and made one or more changes, resulting in tree N+1.

We can think of a delta as a list of changes which express the difference between two trees. This includes files or directories that have been added, modified, renamed, deleted, or moved.

The delta concept can be used for individual files as well. A file delta merely expresses the difference between two files. Once again, the reason we calculate a file delta is because we believe it will be smaller, usually because one of the files is derived from the other.

Many modern version control tools use binary file deltas for repository storage. One popular file delta algorithm is called vcdiff[1]. It outputs a list of byte ranges which have been changed. This means it can handle any kind of file, binary or text. As an ancillary benefit, the vcdiff algorithm compresses the data at the same time.

Binary deltas are a helpful feature for some version control tool users, especially in situations where the binary files are large. Consider the case where a user checks out a 500 MB file, changes a few bytes, and commits it back in. If the repository is using file deltas, it will only grow by a small amount.

Some version control tools can also use binary deltas to improve performance over slow network lines. If both sides of the network connection already have version N, then

---

[1]http://tools.ietf.org/html/rfc3284

transferring version N+1 over the wire can be accomplished by sending just a delta. The increase in network performance for offsite users can be quite dramatic.

2. Git: Cryptographic Hashes

Most DVCS tools, including Git, Mercurial, and Veracity, use cryptographic hashes.

A cryptographic hash is an algorithm which constructs a short *digest* from a sequence of bytes of any length. There are many such hash algorithms[2]. For the SHA-1[3] algorithm, the output digest is always 160 bits in length. Some hash algorithms, including SHA-2[4] and Skein[5], are capable of generating longer digests, at lengths of 256, 512, or even 1024 bits.

2.1. Example with SHA-1

Let's take a closer look at how a DVCS makes use of cryptographic hashes. I will be using Git for my examples in this section, but it applies to Veracity as well. Mercurial, on the other hand, does things a bit differently.

In this example, we want to use our VCS to store four text files. For the sake of keeping things simple, each file is just a few bytes long. (The example would be more realistic if the files were a lot bigger, but you get the idea.)

```
eric:hashes_example eric$ echo Eric > file1.txt

eric:hashes_example eric$ echo Erik > file2.txt

eric:hashes_example eric$ echo eric > file3.txt

eric:hashes_example eric$ echo Eirc > file4.txt

eric:hashes_example eric$ ls -l
total 32
-rw-r--r--  1 eric  staff  5 Jun 20 10:29 file1.txt
-rw-r--r--  1 eric  staff  5 Jun 20 10:29 file2.txt
-rw-r--r--  1 eric  staff  5 Jun 20 10:29 file3.txt
-rw-r--r--  1 eric  staff  5 Jun 20 10:29 file4.txt
```

---

[2]http://en.wikipedia.org/wiki/Cryptographic_hash_function
[3]http://en.wikipedia.org/wiki/SHA-1
[4]http://en.wikipedia.org/wiki/SHA-2
[5]http://en.wikipedia.org/wiki/Skein_(hash_function)

Each of these files contains my first name or a slight misspelling thereof. Now I use Git to show me the SHA-1 hash for each of these files.[6]

```
eric:hashes_example eric$ git hash-object file1.txt
44bf09d0a2c36585aed1c34ba2e5d958a9379718

eric:hashes_example eric$ git hash-object file2.txt
63ae94dae6067d9683cc3a9cea87f8fb388c0e80

eric:hashes_example eric$ git hash-object file3.txt
782d09e3fbfd8cf1b5c13f3eb9621362f9089ed5

eric:hashes_example eric$ git hash-object file4.txt
a627820d67e455a4f0dfa49c912fbddb88fca483
```

Note that even though all four of the input strings are similar, the resulting hash values are very different. As you'll see later, this is important.

Git uses hashes in two important ways.

+ When you commit a file into your repository, Git calculates and remembers the hash of the contents of the file. When you later retrieve the file, Git can verify that the hash of the data being retrieved exactly matches the hash that was computed when it was stored. In this fashion, the hash serves as an integrity checksum, ensuring that the data has not been corrupted or altered.

  For example, if somebody were to hack the DVCS repository such that the contents of file2.txt were changed to "Fred", retrieval of that file would cause an error because the software would detect that the SHA-1 digest for "Fred" is not 63ae94dae606...

+ Git also uses hash digests as database keys for looking up files and data.

  If you ask Git for the contents of file2.txt, it will first look up its previously computed digest for the contents of that file[7], which is 63ae94dae606... Then it looks in the repository for the data associated with that value and returns "Erik" as the result. (For the moment, you should try to ignore the fact that we just used a 40 character hex string as the database key for four characters of data.)

Let's assume that we now want to add another file, file5.txt, which happens to contain exactly the same string as file2.txt. So the hash of the file contents will be exactly the same.

---

[6]Actually, Git prepends a short header (blob <filesize>\0) when it calculates SHA-1 values.
[7]Git stores this information in a structure called a "tree" object.

```
eric:hashes_example eric$ echo Erik > file5.txt

eric:hashes_example eric$ git hash-object file5.txt
63ae94dae6067d9683cc3a9cea87f8fb388c0e80
```

When Git stores the contents of file5.txt, it will realize that it already has a copy of that data. There is no need to store it again. Hooray! Git just saved us four bytes of storage space! (Keep in mind that instead of "Erik", these two files could contain a gigabyte of video, which would imply a somewhat more motivating space savings.) This process is called *deduplication*.

This is deeply neato, but what would have happened if file5.txt did not contain "Erik" but somehow happened to still have a SHA-1 hash of 63ae94dae606…? According to the pigeonhole principle[8], this is theoretically possible. When a cryptographic hash algorithm generates the same digest for two different pieces of data, we call that a *collision*.

If a collision were to happen in this situation, we would have some pretty big problems. When the DVCS is asked to store the contents of file5.txt (which does not contain "Erik" but which somehow **does** have a SHA-1 hash of 63ae94dae606…), it would incorrectly conclude that it already has a copy of that data. So the real contents of file5.txt would be discarded. Future attempts to retrieve the contents of that file would erroneously return "Erik".

Because of this, it is rather important that the DVCS never encounter two different pieces of data which have the same digest. Fortunately, good cryptographic hash functions are designed to make such collisions **extremely** unlikely.

And just how unlikely is that?

2.2. Collisions

Your chances of winning the Powerball lottery are **far** better than finding a hash collision. After all, lotteries often have actual winners. The probability of a hash collision is more like a lottery that has been running since prehistoric times and has never had a winner and will probably not have a winner for billions of years.

It is no accident that "Eric", "Erik", "eric", and "Eirc" have hash values that are so different. Cryptographic hash algorithms are intentionally designed to ensure that two similar pieces of data have digests which are not similar.

The likelihood of accidentally finding a collision is related to the bit length of the hash. Specifically, the average number of evaluations necessary to find a collision is

---

[8]http://en.wikipedia.org/wiki/Pigeonhole_principle

$2^{(\text{bit\_length}/2)}$.[9] So, if we are trying to find two pieces of data which have the same SHA-1 hash, we could expect to be searching through 2^{80} pieces of data. If we check one million hashes per second, we'll probably find a collision in about 38 billion years.

Unsurprisingly, no one has ever found a SHA-1 collision.

Note that these probabilities apply to the situation where a hash collision is found accidentally, roughly equivalent to the notion of somebody who is just checking random combinations to see if a collision happens to show up. But what if somebody is being a bit more intentional, searching for a collision using a better method than just being random? Surely this search won't take as long if we're being smart about it, right?

Well, no. That's part of the definition of a good cryptographic hash algorithm: There **is** no better method. If there were, then the hash would be considered "broken".

This is fairly important for a DVCS. For example, consider the situation where somebody has access to a repository containing source code for a payroll system. Their goal is to alter the source code such that they will get extra money on payday.

If they can take a source file and then find an altered version of that file which has the same SHA-1 hash, they might be able to achieve their goal. Because the SHA-1 hash matches, it is quite likely that they could store their altered version in the repository without anyone noticing.

But with a strong cryptographic hash function, it is virtually impossible to find **any** string of bytes which have the same SHA-1 hash as the original file. And it is even less likely that they could find an altered version which accomplishes the goal of giving them more money, or even compiles without errors.

Incidentally, SHA-1 is actually considered broken. For security-oriented applications, it is obsolete and should generally not be used anymore. However, let me explain a bit more about what cryptographers mean when they say that SHA-1 is broken.

SHA-1 is considered broken because somebody found a smarter way to search for a collision, a method which is more effective than just trying random combinations over and over as fast as you can. But that doesn't mean that finding a collision is easy. It simply means that the search for a collision in SHA-1 should take less time than it is theoretically supposed to take. Instead of the full 80 bits of strength that we would expect SHA-1 to have, it actually has about 51 bits of strength. That means that instead of 38 billion years, we should expect to find a collision in about 70 years.

---

[9]http://en.wikipedia.org/wiki/Birthday_problem

But still, 70 years is a long time. It remains the case that nobody has ever found a collision in SHA-1.

Nonetheless, there are some who will feel safer using a stronger hash algorithm. This is why we decided to give Veracity support for SHA-2 and Skein, both of which allow for 256 bits or more and neither of which has been broken. At 256 bits, the search for a collision is going to take a **long** time. Instead of one million attempts per second, let's do a trillion. And let's assume that there are 6 billion people on Earth and every one of them has a computer and each of us are doing a trillion checks per second. At that rate, it should take us around 2 trillion years to find a collision.

3. Mercurial: Repository Structure

3.1. Revlogs

An important part of Mercurial's design is the notion of a *revlog*, a file format which is designed to store all versions of a given file in an efficient manner. Mercurial uses the revlog format for basically everything it stores in the repository.

Each revision of a file is identified by a "NodeID", which is a SHA-1/160 hash of its contents (combined with the position of that node in the history).

Each version of the file can be stored as either a complete snapshot of the file's contents, or as a binary delta against the previous version. Mercurial stores a complete snapshot every so often to ensure that it is only necessary to walk back so far.

The revlog file is append-only. Each new version of an object is written to the end of the file without altering anything that was already there. This means that it uses forward deltas. Reverse deltas are a lot more typical today, because the most common operation is the retrieval of the most recent version. With reverse deltas the most recent version is always stored as a snapshot. In Mercurial, retrieving the most recent version might involve reconstructing it from an older snapshot with later deltas applied to it.

Reading a given version of the file from a revlog can be accomplished by a single contiguous read. No seeks are necessary. If that version is stored as a snapshot, just read it. If it is stored as a delta, read it and any deltas before it, back to the previous snapshot. This elegant aspect of the design is one of the reasons Mercurial is so fast.

A revlog is actually two files. The .d file contains the actual file data. The .i file is an index designed to make it easier to find things. When the revlog is small, these two files are combined into one, with the data stored in the .i file and no .d file.

As I said, Mercurial gets a lot of its efficiency from the careful design of this revlog file format, but there are some tradeoffs. Mercurial always assumes that the entire file (including the last snapshot and all deltas) will fit into RAM. This makes things much faster, but it makes Mercurial generally not effective for large files (over 10 MB).[10]

```
lottery harry$ hg debugindex .hg/store/data/src/pb.c.i
  rev    offset  length   base linkrev nodeid        p1           p2
    0         0     467      0      10 a7bdd2379025 000000000000 000000000000
    1       467     168      0      12 692932a95c0d 000000000000 a7bdd2379025
    2       635     173      0      15 f1d9cb4201e4 692932a95c0d 000000000000
    3       808     476      0      17 d238a6113e4c f1d9cb4201e4 000000000000
    4      1284     491      0      18 b71d299270a5 f1d9cb4201e4 000000000000
    5      1775     470      0      19 4a7ebb32f962 b71d299270a5 d238a6113e4c
    6      2245      64      0      20 6b99ca4dde14 4a7ebb32f962 000000000000
    7      2309     177      0      21 33557d969679 d238a6113e4c 000000000000
    8      2486     213      0      22 e4d67566afd0 6b99ca4dde14 33557d969679
    9      2699     102      0      23 ab4bcfb966f8 33557d969679 000000000000
   10      2801     384      0      24 86d19e47e6d0 e4d67566afd0 000000000000
   11      3185      88      0      25 4969c00e0bc8 86d19e47e6d0 ab4bcfb966f8
```

```
lottery harry$ hg debugindex .hg/store/00manifest.i
  rev    offset  length   base linkrev nodeid        p1           p2
    0         0      52      0       0 4bf51ef87fa1 000000000000 000000000000
    1        52      52      1       1 df9a6175c86f 4bf51ef87fa1 000000000000
    2       104      52      2       2 f282fd300cae 4bf51ef87fa1 000000000000
    3       156      52      3       3 2128ed694101 df9a6175c86f f282fd300cae
    4       208      52      4       4 cf6095e27d1b 2128ed694101 000000000000
    5       260      52      5       5 a3954dc14901 2128ed694101 000000000000
    6       312      52      6       6 84f3337a15c2 cf6095e27d1b a3954dc14901
    7       364      56      7       7 723f96182c10 84f3337a15c2 000000000000
    8       420      52      8       8 f81e41ac9f78 84f3337a15c2 000000000000
    9       472      56      9       9 43b4d425d11b f81e41ac9f78 723f96182c10
   10       528     100      9      10 db730b6b114f 43b4d425d11b 000000000000
   11       628      56     11      11 c0916422f5f9 43b4d425d11b 000000000000
   12       684      98     11      12 a0a068b209a9 c0916422f5f9 db730b6b114f
   13       782   12861     11      13 fa7d4fbf3283 a0a068b209a9 000000000000
   14     13643      91     14      14 847ed0078d54 fa7d4fbf3283 000000000000
   15     13734      62     14      15 26f762825d61 847ed0078d54 000000000000
   16     13796      61     14      16 fa14759e626d 26f762825d61 000000000000
   17     13857      62     14      17 65ed8051c722 fa14759e626d 000000000000
   18     13919     122     18      18 96c0a3cf81b1 fa14759e626d 000000000000
   19     14041      62     18      19 61aa1de12abe 96c0a3cf81b1 65ed8051c722
   20     14103      62     18      20 f68d6078c862 61aa1de12abe 000000000000
   21     14165     119     21      21 47f22792ec34 65ed8051c722 000000000000
   22     14284      62     21      22 1e7caebb4684 f68d6078c862 47f22792ec34
   23     14346      62     21      23 a30745ba5cae 47f22792ec34 000000000000
   24     14408     119     24      24 cbe36265b98c 1e7caebb4684 000000000000
   25     14527      62     24      25 f991d0456dd4 cbe36265b98c a30745ba5cae
```

---

[10]There is a Bigfiles extension which works around the problem by keeping the large file somewhere else and storing a reference to it.

3.2. Manifests

For every version of the tree, Mercurial stores a *manifest*, a complete list of all the files in the tree and their versions.

```
lottery harry$ hg debugdata .hg/store/00manifest.i 24
.hgtagsc04bfcf9c20c06746293f5474da270d88501a9c1
Makefileb87f10c1ca797b426bc6ac4522aae0de1bf6902a
src/pb.c86d19e47e6d07cfddba6a4a7f6d7013dd782075a
```

The manifest is also stored in a revlog. The deltification here is critical because storing a full listing for every revision of the tree could become enormously large.

Note that a Mercurial manifest only contains files. Mercurial does not track information about the directories that contain those files. Consequently, it cannot store an empty directory.

3.3. Changesets

For each revision of the tree, Mercurial stores a changeset. A changeset is a record which lists all the changes to files, including who made the change, the log message, the date/time, and the name of the branch.

```
lottery harry$ hg debugdata .hg/store/00changelog.i 24
cbe36265b98c1f656ad1f0c3546c458a68ee85eb
Harry <harry@futilisoft.com>
1305662021 18000
src/pb.c

fixed spelling error
```

A Mercurial changeset has zero, one, or two parents. If it is the root node of the DAG, it has zero parents. If it is a merge node, it has two parents. All the rest of the nodes have one parent.

The SHA-1/160 hash of the changeset record becomes the changeset ID.

All changesets are stored in the *changelog*, which is another revlog file.

4. Veracity: DAGs and Data

Veracity is written in C (the core libraries) and JavaScript (the web applications). It is primarily a command-line application (vv) but also contains a built-in web server and web-based user interface.

I am using Veracity for version control as I write this book. So in the following examples, I'm just going to crawl through the guts of my book repository. A little information up-front:

+ The Veracity scripting interpreter is called **vscript**. The scripting language is JavaScript, extended with a bunch of hooks into the Veracity libraries.

+ The name of my repository instance is book2.

+ In general, Veracity stores everything in JSON.

4.1. DAGs and Blobs

A Veracity repository stores two kinds of things: DAGs and blobs. First let's talk about DAGs.

A DAG is used to represent the version history of something. Each node of the DAG represents one version, with one or more arrows pointing to the version(s) from which that node was derived. A DAG has one root node.[11] If a DAG has just one leaf node, then we know without ambiguity which version is the latest.

Veracity supports two kinds of DAGs:

+ A *tree* DAG keeps the version history of a directory structure from a filesystem. Each node of the DAG represents one version of the whole tree.

+ A *database* (or "db") DAG keeps the version history of a database, or a list of records. Each node of the DAG represents one state of the complete database.

A repository can have many database DAGs, each with a different purpose, distinguished by a numeric ID we call a dagnum.

Here's a vscript snippet which lists all the DAGs in a repository:

```
var r = sg.open_repo("book2");
var a = r.list_dags();
r.close();
print(sg.to_json__pretty_print(a));
```

When I run this script, I get:

---

[11]Git allows the DAG to have multiple root nodes. Veracity does not.

```
eric:~ eric$ vscript list_dags.js
[
    "0000000010101042",
    "0000000010101052",
    "0000000010102062",
    "0000000010102072",
    "0000000010201001",
    "0000000010201011",
    "00000000102021c2",
    "00000000102021d2",
    "00000000102031c2",
    "00000000102031d2",
    "00000000102040c2",
    "00000000102040d2",
    "00000000102051c2",
    "00000000102051d2",
    "00000000102071c2",
    "00000000102071d2",
    "0000000010301002",
    "0000000010301012",
    "0000000010302002",
    "0000000010302012"
]
```

Well, that's not very friendly, is it? All those hex numbers! And how can there be 20 DAGs in this repository, anyway?

Actually, there are only 10. Sort of. What we've got here are 10 "real" DAGs, each of which has an audit DAG.

For every changeset in every non-audit DAG, an audit record is added (to its audit DAG) containing the UTC timestamp (on the local machine) and the userid of who committed it.

If you look closely, the audit DAGs are evident here because they're the ones where the second digit (from the right) is an odd number.

The purpose of each DAG can be found by looking at the bits in the dagnum while reading a particularly tedious section of the Veracity source code. I'll spare you the trouble. Here is a description of all 10 DAGs:

dagnum	Description
0000000010101042	Areas (db)
0000000010102062	Users (db)
0000000010201001	Version control (tree)
00000000102021c2	VC Comments (db)

dagnum	Description
00000000102031c2	VC Stamps (db)
00000000102040c2	VC Tags (db)
00000000102051c2	VC Named branches (db)
00000000102071c2	VC Hooks (db)
0000000010301002	Work items (db)
0000000010302002	Builds (db)

As you can see, the db DAGs have the tree DAG outnumbered, 9 to 1. In fact, those 10 audit DAGs are db DAGs as well. So we've got 19 db DAGs and 1 tree DAG. This is fairly typical for a Veracity repository. The source tree itself is filesystem-oriented data, but most other data fits better into a record-with-fields design. Veracity uses db DAGs to track lots of different stuff.

Six of the DAGs in this list are related to version control. There is the tree itself, and then we have one DAG each to keep track of comments, stamps, tags, named branches, and hooks.

The users DAG is used to keep track of user accounts. The areas DAG can be used to keep track of which DAGs logically go together. All six of the version control (VC) DAGs are in one area. Work items and builds are another area.

Before we go on, we should tidy up a bit. We've got enough big long hex numbers around, so let's get rid of the ones for the dagnums. The scripting API has defined constants for all the primary dagnums.

```
eric:~ eric$ vscript
vscript> print(sg.dagnum.VERSION_CONTROL)
0000000010201001
vscript> ^D
```

Now let's dive into the version control DAG itself. The way a DAG works is that the most recent information is in the leaves. Here's a little script to list all the leaf nodes for the version control tree DAG:

```
var r = sg.open_repo("book2");
var leaves = r.fetch_dag_leaves(sg.dagnum.VERSION_CONTROL);
r.close();
print(sg.to_json__pretty_print(leaves));
```

Running the script, I get one result, indicating that my repository has no branching going on:

```
eric:~ eric$ vscript fetch_dag_leaves.js
[
    "f10628e5792251dc886f600a6ae8610a38ac2204"
]
```

The ID of a dagnode is also the ID of its changeset blob. Which reminds me, let's talk about blobs.

A blob is just a sequence of bytes. It can be empty, or it can have many gigabytes in it. The length of a blob is represented as a 64-bit integer, so Veracity can handle any size blob you've got.

A repository provides key-value storage for blobs. The key for each blob is the cryptographic hash of its contents. The repository in this example is configured to use SHA-1, the same hash function used by Mercurial and Git.

In the Veracity code, we use the word *HID*, short for "hash ID", to refer to the hash of a blob.

Whenever you retrieve a blob (in full), the HID is verified.

There are two kinds of blobs.

- ◆ User data. Every file you store under version control becomes a blob. Actually each version of that file becomes a blob.
- ◆ Program data. Program data is used to store things that Veracity needs to remember, such as the contents of a directory, or database records, or changeset objects. All program data is stored as JSON.

When creating a new changeset in a DAG, we create a serialized changeset record. The HID of that record becomes the ID of the new dagnode.

4.2. Changesets

So, when we ask for the dagnode IDs for the leaf nodes, the resulting IDs can be used to retrieve the changeset blob. Here is what that changeset blob looks like:

```
eric:book2 eric$ vv dump_json f10628e5792251dc886f600a6ae8610a38ac2204
{
  "dagnum" : "0000000010201001",
  "generation" : 91,
  "parents" :
  [
    "c821cfbc8964db9958d1278a5e4e2947462730e9"
  ],
```

```
"tree" :
{
  "changes" :
  {
    "c821cfbc8964db9958d1278a5e4e2947462730e9" :
    {
      "g3a3b61269bea4392951a785dcf7efbde40e5331a56db11e0a84b60fb42f09aca" :
      {
        "hid" : "40c1af01a8c0cea66ecb99529befbd8e7a004c42"
      },
      "g8a7471f886864c04a836d0c4621df781a2e67bbe572611e08f5d60fb42f09aca" :
      {
        "hid" : "a3656282d8c467f00b21d83317d2de0374af761c"
      }
    }
  },
  "root" : "c86c077f1f0c165f90ca7715b4a41d8281fc5feb"
},
"ver" : 1
}
```

As I mentioned before, there are two kinds of DAGs, db and tree. The version control DAG is, of course, a tree DAG, so its changeset records have a "tree" section. The db changesets look a little different as you'll see later.

- dagnum identifies the DAG to which this changeset belongs.

- generation is an integer which indicates the distance from this dagnode to the root. The root dagnode has a generation of 1. All other nodes have a generation which is 1 + the maximum generation of its parents.

- ver defines the version number of the format of the changeset record.

- parents is an array of references to the parents of this dagnode.

- tree.changes contains one entry for each parent. Each such entry contains a list of everything in this dagnode which has changed with respect to that parent.

- tree.root contains the HID of the treenode for the root of the tree.

So, what's a treenode?

4.3. Treenodes

In a version control tree, each of the user's files is stored as a blob. But each directory is a treenode. Here's one:

```
eric:book2 eric$ vv dump_json c86c077f1f0c165f90ca7715b4a41d8281fc5feb | expand -t 2
{
  "tne" :
  {
    "g3a3b61269bea4392951a785dcf7efbde40e5331a56db11e0a84b60fb42f09aca" :
    {
      "hid" : "40c1af01a8c0cea66ecb99529befbd8e7a004c42",
      "name" : "@",
      "type" : 2
    }
  },
  "ver" : 1
}
```

This treenode is actually what we call the "super-root". It's an extra level of tree hierarchy that the user never sees, so that we can record metadata about the user's root. So let's dive one level deeper.

```
eric:book2 eric$ vv dump_json 40c1af01a8c0cea66ecb99529befbd8e7a004c42 | expand -t 2
{
  "tne" :
  {
    "g0ae054064de54d4b88db6d8b26ad4d79688421e0595811e0804960fb42f09aca" :
    {
      "bits" : 1,
      "hid" : "56eedb1343e12183875d14a1ec3d1a4098d49a25",
      "name" : "g",
      "type" : 1
    },
    "g8a7471f886864c04a836d0c4621df781a2e67bbe572611e08f5d60fb42f09aca" :
    {
      "hid" : "a3656282d8c467f00b21d83317d2de0374af761c",
      "name" : "version_control_howto.xml",
      "type" : 1
    },
    "g8e481f4af9d5450a83fc77cca7f0bc07a70fdfa466e511e0837160fb42f09aca" :
    {
      "hid" : "9e65873dbc6d7c8579392a6acc9a856d25bb0c46",
      "name" : "docbook-xsl-1.76.1",
      "type" : 2
    },
    "gb45372a549bb4044b65b788212d0828af338a140580311e08ced60fb42f09aca" :
    {
      "hid" : "85e06e062d72def73dce1897bdcef9531ec87526",
      "name" : "images",
      "type" : 2
    },
    "ge502a109a22e44c099d66014fb5ecd1d9477f9025d3b11e0b7a360fb42f09aca" :
    {
      "hid" : "19ba6f1d215bfad27181c4113ce80985dae7fdeb",
      "name" : "custom_fo.xsl",
      "type" : 1
```

```
      }
    },
    "ver" : 1
}
```

This is a more illustrative treenode. Basically its tne object (short for tree node entry) contains a list of entries, one for each item in the directory.

This directory has five entries in it:

+ g is a bash script I use to generate a PDF.
+ version_control_howto.xml is the DocBook file containing all my content.
+ docbook-xsl-1.76.1 is a copy of the DocBook XSL stylesheets.
+ images is a subdirectory containing all the artwork for the book.
+ custom_fo.xsl is my XSL customization layer.

For each entry, the treenode knows the HID of the blob containing the contents of that item. In the case of a file, such as custom_fo.xsl, the HID refers to the blob that contains the actual contents of the file. In the case of a subdirectory like images, the HID refers to another treenode.

The blob a3656282d8c467f00b21d83317d2de0374af761c contains (one version of) the DocBook content of this book.

4.4. DB Records

So where's the log message on this commit? For that we have to look in a different DAG. Using the same technique as above, we find that the leaf for the version control comments DAG is 053da8cbbd986b14dc06b3d8dab08be3388266ff. Let's dump that changeset and see what it looks like.

```
eric:book2 eric$ vv dump_json 053da8cbbd986b14dc06b3d8dab08be3388266ff | expand -t 2
{
  "dagnum" : "00000000102021c2",
  "db" :
  {
    "changes" :
    {
      "9ff7c857361d30d6a51b9fcf9f5ddbff9940d4e1" :
      {
        "add" :
        {
          "fb96b2c70dcca6a82e6b8ee222c26395cccf4d42" : 0
        }
      }
```

```
      }
   },
   "generation" : 91,
   "parents" :
   [
      "9ff7c857361d30d6a51b9fcf9f5ddbff9940d4e1"
   ],
   "ver" : 1
}
```

This is a db changeset instead of a tree changeset. It contains a "db" section, which, again, contains one delta against each parent. That delta indicates that one new record was added. Let's dump the blob for the new record and see what it looks like.

```
eric:book2 eric$ vv dump_json fb96b2c70dcca6a82e6b8ee222c26395cccf4d42 | expand -t 2
{
   "csid" : "f10628e5792251dc886f600a6ae8610a38ac2204",
   "text" : "committing my changes before I continue writing"[12]
}
```

And there's the db record for the comment. Note that the csid field matches the changeset ID from the version control DAG.

What about the who and when? Once again, we need to check another DAG, the audit DAG for the version control DAG. Its dagnum is 0000000010201011. I grab its only leaf and dump the corresponding changeset record:

```
eric:book2 eric$ vv dump_json 15bc2d16081d6ad6baeb4c790821d8aeee864d34 | expand -t 2
{
   "dagnum" : "0000000010201011",
   "db" :
   {
      "changes" :
      {
         "3a4b6f6222d5ae761ad375eb1c7aa8a5f9ba0390" :
         {
            "add" :
            {
               "c52ff03833aeb8f180583ce2fc7ea7bbf7e392bf" : 0
            }
         }
      }
   },
   "generation" : 92,
   "parents" :
   [
```

---

[12]This brief, content-free log message was not a shining example of best practices.

```
    "3a4b6f6222d5ae761ad375eb1c7aa8a5f9ba0390"
  ],
  "ver" : 1
}
```

Here is the new record:

```
eric:book2 eric$ vv dump_json c52ff03833aeb8f180583ce2fc7ea7bbf7e392bf | expand -t 2
{
  "csid" : "f10628e5792251dc886f600a6ae8610a38ac2204",
  "timestamp" : "1304457549322",
  "userid" : "gc580073ae5164a61bd92c3241bf3d9f457b0b01056db11e0995060fb42f09aca"
}
```

The value for userid isn't very intuitive, is it? That is actually the record ID for the user record, located over in a separate DAG.

Here is a script to dump all user records:

```
eric:~ eric$ cat u.js
var repo = sg.open_repo("book2");
var zs = new zingdb(repo, sg.dagnum.USERS);
var recs = zs.query('user', ['*']);
repo.close();
print(sg.to_json__pretty_print(recs));
```

Running the script produces the following output:

```
eric:~ eric$ vscript u.js | expand -t 2
[
  {
    "name" : "eric",
    "prefix" : "X",
    "recid" : "gc580073ae5164a61bd92c3241bf3d9f457b0b01056db11e0995060fb42f09aca"
  }
]
```

So at last you can see that it was me who did the commit shown above.

4.5. Templates

Now let's dive a bit deeper. A db DAG contains a "database", or a set of records. These records must follow a template. That template is basically like a schema for the database. It describes one or more record types, specifying the fields for each record type.

Here is the template for the version control comments DAG:

```
{
    "version" : 1,
    "rectypes" :
    {
        "item" :
        {
            "fields" :
            {
                "csid" :
                {
                    "datatype" : "string",
                    "constraints" :
                    {
                        "required" : true,
                        "index" : true
                    }
                },
                "text" :
                {
                    "datatype" : "string",
                    "constraints" :
                    {
                        "required" : true,
                        "maxlength" : 16384,
                        "full_text_search" : true
                    }
                }
            }
        }
    }
}
```

It is illegal to have a template where merge can fail. The template above satisfies that rule because it has no record ID, which means that records cannot be modified and that unique constraints are not allowed. This template is a rather simplistic example.

Here's a slightly more complicated example, the template for version control tags:

```
{
    "version" : 1,
    "rectypes" :
    {
        "item" :
        {
        "merge" :
            {
                "merge_type" : "field",
                "auto" :
                [
                    {
                        "op" : "most_recent"
                    }
```

```
            ]
        },
        "fields" :
        {
            "csid" :
            {
                "datatype" : "string",
                "constraints" :
                {
                    "required" : true,
                    "index" : true
                }
            },
            "tag" :
            {
                "datatype" : "string",
                "constraints" :
                {
                    "required" : true,
                    "index" : true,
                    "unique" : true,
                    "maxlength" : 256
                },
                "merge" :
                {
                    "uniqify" :
                    {
                        "op" : "append_userprefix_unique",
                        "num_digits" : 2,
                        "which" : "least_impact"
                    }
                }
            }
        }
    }
}
```

Like a comment, a tag has just two fields: The changeset ID to which it applies and a string. But for a tag, that string is required to be unique, which introduces the possibility that the unique constraint could be violated on a merge. So Veracity requires us to provide a way to *uniqify*, to resolve the violation of the unique constraint automatically as the merge is happening.

4.6. Repository Storage

Now let's look at how all this stuff is actually stored.

The repository API presents an abstraction of a repository instance. Callers of the API remain unaware of certain details of exactly how dagnodes and blobs are being stored.

These details are left to the storage implementation, thus allowing different tradeoffs to be used for different situations.

In Veracity 1.0, the only shipping implementation of this repository API is called FS3. The "FS" stands for "filesystem", representing the fact that blobs are simply stored in files (although not one blob per file). The "3" simply means that it is the third incarnation—FS1 and FS2 did not survive the development process.

FS3 stores repositories in the "closet", which by default is a directory in your home directory named .sgcloset.

```
eric:book2 eric$ cd ~/.sgcloset/

eric:.sgcloset eric$ ls -l
total 496
-rw-r--r--  1 eric  staff    60416 May  3 18:02 descriptors.jsondb
drwxr-xr-x  4 eric  staff      136 May  3 18:02 repo
-rw-r--r--  1 eric  staff   190464 Apr 24 19:35 settings.jsondb

eric:.sgcloset eric$ cd repo

eric:repo eric$ ls -l
total 0
drwxr-xr-x  22 eric  staff  748 May  3 15:04 alpo_858b
drwxr-xr-x  16 eric  staff  544 May  3 18:00 book2_d2a1

eric:repo eric$ cd book2_d2a1/

eric:book2_d2a1 eric$ ls -l
total 771928
-rw-r--r--  1 eric  staff      20480 Mar 25 07:28 0000000010101042.dbndx
-rw-r--r--  1 eric  staff      28672 Mar 25 07:28 0000000010102062.dbndx
-rw-r--r--  1 eric  staff    3390464 May  3 16:19 0000000010201001.treendx
-rw-r--r--  1 eric  staff      58368 May  3 16:19 0000000010201011.dbndx
-rw-r--r--  1 eric  staff     118784 May  3 16:19 00000000102021c2.dbndx
-rw-r--r--  1 eric  staff      19456 Mar 25 07:28 00000000102031c2.dbndx
-rw-r--r--  1 eric  staff      21504 Mar 25 07:28 00000000102040c2.dbndx
-rw-r--r--  1 eric  staff      75776 May  3 16:19 00000000102051c2.dbndx
-rw-r--r--  1 eric  staff      18432 Mar 25 07:28 00000000102071c2.dbndx
-rw-r--r--  1 eric  staff      99328 Mar 25 07:28 0000000010301002.dbndx
-rw-r--r--  1 eric  staff      58368 Mar 25 07:28 0000000010302002.dbndx
-rw-r--r--  1 eric  staff  390010297 May  3 16:19 (000001)
drwxr-xr-x  62 eric  staff       2108 May  3 16:19 f
-rw-r--r--  1 eric  staff    1283072 May  3 16:19 (fs3.sqlite3)
```

These files are my book repository. Actually, two of them matter more than the others.

- All the blobs are stored in the file called 000001. FS3 stores blobs by appending them to this file. When the file gets to be a gigabyte, it starts a new file called 000002.

Reflecting a strong bias toward reliability, the FS3 data file is append-only. Once a blob has been appended, it is never altered. Furthermore, Veracity's repository API has no way to remove a blob or a dagnode.

+ The other important file is `fs3.sqlite3`. As its name suggests, this is a SQLite[13] database. It contains two things:

    + The list of blobs, and for each blob, the offset/length of where to find it in the data file.

    + The list of dagnodes.

All of the other files in the repository directory are somewhat secondary.

Most of them are repository indexes, with file names ending in `ndx`. We can think of these in the same way that we think about indexes in a SQL database. They do not contain actual data; they exist simply to make certain operations faster. It is possible to delete all the repository indexes and reconstruct them using nothing more than the data file(s) and the `fs3.sqlite3` file.

Note that in some situations it is legal for a Veracity repository instance to have no indexes at all. This capability is helpful for setting up a very scalable central server.

For Veracity 1.0, repository indexes are not transferred by clone, push, or pull. Each repository instance is responsible for maintaining its own indexes.

4.7. Blob Encodings

The Veracity repository API allows a blob to be stored in one of three "encodings".

+ full — the exact bytes of the blob are all stored

+ zlib — the blob is stored compressed

+ vcdiff — the blob is stored as a vcdiff delta relative to another blob

For performance, FS3 stores all incoming new blobs in the zlib encoding.

Once the blob is stored in a given repository instance, its encoding cannot be changed. But its encoding **can** be altered in the course of a clone operation. While the clone command copies the blob from one instance of the repository to another, it can re-encode the blob as it passes through. For example, the following Veracity command produces a deltified copy of a repository by using the --pack option with the clone command.

---

[13]`http://www.sqlite.org/`

```
~ harry$ vv clone --pack lottery lottery_deltified
```

And that reminds me that I should say a word or two about Veracity's implementation of the communication between repository instances.

Similar to the repository API, another API is used to hide the details for clone, push, and pull. Veracity currently includes two implementations of this API, one for local operations and one which works over HTTP.

By default, clone, push, and pull always transfer blobs without changing the encoding. This means that if a blob is in deltified (vcdiff) form, it will be transferred over the network in that form, thus saving network traffic.

13   Best Practices

I close this book with some general advice for effective software development using version control.

1. Run diff just before you commit, every time

Never commit your changes without giving them a quick review in some sort of diff tool.

2. Read the diffs from other developers too

Every morning before you start your own coding tasks, use your favorite diff tool[1] to look at all the changes that everybody else checked in the day before. Many of the best developers I have known make this a habit.

When you read the diffs, two good things might happen:

1. The code might get better. Reading the diffs is like an informal code review. You might find something that needs to be fixed.

2. You might learn something. Maybe one of your coworkers is using a technique you don't know about. Or maybe reading the diffs simply gives you a deeper understanding of the project you are working on.

3. Keep your repositories as small as possible

And no smaller.

Since the DVCS model involves every developer keeping a complete copy of the repository on her desktop machine, it is best to be intentional about how much stuff goes

---

[1]http://www.sourcegear.com/diffmerge/—Your favorite diff tool is SourceGear DiffMerge, right? :-)

into a single repository. It is **not** a good idea for a large corporation to have just one repository into which all projects go.

4. Group your commits logically

Each changeset you commit to the repository should correspond to one task. A "task" might be a bug-fix or a feature. Include all of the repository changes which were necessary to complete that task and nothing else. Avoid fixing multiple unrelated bugs in a single changeset.

5. Explain your commits completely

Every version control tool provides a way to include a log message (a comment) when committing changes to the repository. This comment is important. If we consistently use good comments when we commit, our repository's history contains not only every change we have ever made, but it also contains an explanation of why those changes happened. These kinds of records can be invaluable later as we forget things.

I believe developers should be encouraged to enter log messages which are as long as necessary to explain what is going on. Don't just type "minor change". Tell us what the minor change was. Don't just tell us "fixed bug 1234". Tell us what bug 1234 is and tell us a little bit about the changes that were necessary to fix it.

6. Only store the canonical stuff

People sometimes ask us what kind of things can be stored in a repository. In general, the answer is: "Any file". It is true that this book is focused on tools which are designed for software developers. However, any modern VCS doesn't really care about what kinds of files it is asked to store.

Although you **can** store anything you want in a repository, that doesn't mean you should. The best practice here is to store everything which is created manually, and nothing else. I call this "the canonical stuff".

Do not store any file which is automatically generated. Store your hand-edited source code. Don't store EXEs and DLLs. If you use a code generation tool, store the input file, not the generated code file. If you generate your product documentation in several different formats, store the original format, the one that you manually edit.

If you have two files, one of which is automatically generated from the other, then you just don't need to store both of them. You would in effect be managing two expressions of the same thing. If one of them gets out of sync with the other, then you have a problem.

7. Don't break the tree

The benefit of working copies is mostly lost if the contents of the repository become "broken". At all times, the contents of the repository should be in a state which allows everyone on the team to continue working. If a developer checks in some code which won't build or won't pass the test suite, the entire team grinds to a halt.

Many teams have some sort of a social penalty which is applied to developers who break the tree. I'm not talking about anything severe, just a little incentive to remind them to be careful. For example, require the guilty party to put a dollar in a glass jar. (Use the money to take the team to go see a movie after the product is shipped.) Another idea is to require the guilty individual to make the coffee every morning. The point is to make the developer feel somewhat embarrassed, but not punished.

Anyway, your central repository is a place you share with the others on your team. Respect them by being careful about what you push there. At a minimum, make sure that stuff builds on your machine before you commit and push. If you have an automated test suite, run it and make sure you didn't break anything.

8. Use tags

Tags are cheap. They don't consume a lot of resources. Your version control tool won't slow down if you use lots of them. Having more tags does not increase your responsibilities. So you can use them as often as you like. The following situations are examples of when you might want to use a tag:

  + When you make a release, apply a tag to the version from which that release was built. A release is the most obvious time to apply a tag. When you release a version of your application to customers, it can be very important to later know exactly which version of the code was released.

+ Sometimes it is necessary to make a change which is widespread or fundamental. Before destabilizing your code, you may want to apply a tag so you can easily find the version just before things started getting messed up.

+ Some automated build systems apply a tag every time a build is done. The usual approach is to first apply the tag and then do a "get by tag" operation to retrieve the code to be used for the build. Using one of these tools can result in an awful lot of tags, but I still like the idea. It eliminates the guesswork of trying to figure out exactly which code was in the build.

9. Always review the merge before you commit.

Successfully using the branching and merging features of your source control tool is first a matter of attitude on the part of the developer. No matter how much help the version control tool provides, it is not as smart as you are. You are responsible for doing the merge. Think of the tool as a tool, not as a consultant.

After your version control tool has done whatever it can do, it's your turn to finish the job. Any conflicts need to be resolved. Make sure the code still builds. Run the unit tests to make sure everything still works. Use a diff tool to review the changes.

Merging branches should always take place in a working copy. Your version control tool should give you a chance to do these checks before you commit the final results of a merge branches operation.

10. Never obliterate anything

Well, almost never.

The purist in me wants to recommend that nothing should ever be obliterated. However, my pragmatic side prevails. There are situations where obliterate is not sinful.

However, obliterate should never be used to delete actual work. Don't obliterate something just because you discovered it was a bad idea. Don't obliterate something just because you don't need it anymore. Obliterate is for situations where something in the repository absolutely must be removed, usually because of legal issues.

11. Don't comment out code

When using a VCS, you shouldn't comment out a big section of code simply because you think you might need it someday. Just delete it. The previous version of the file is still in your version control history, so you can always get it back if and when you need it. This practice is particularly important for web developers, where the commented-out stuff may adversely affect your page load times.

12. Use locks sparingly

It is best to use locks only when you need them. Don't lock files just because you think you **might** need to edit them. Don't lock whole directories—lock only the specific files you need. Don't hold locks any longer than necessary.

13. Build and test your code after every commit

Set up an automated build system which is triggered every time there is a new changeset in the repository instance on your central server. That system should build and test the code, broadcasting a report of the results to the entire team.

Comparison Table

Table A.1. Commands

Operation	Subversion	Mercurial	Git	Veracity
Create	svnadmin create	hg init	git init	vv init
Checkout	svn checkout	[a]	[b]	vv checkout
Commit	svn commit	hg commit	git commit[c]	vv commit
Update	svn update	hg update	git checkout	vv update
Add	svn add	hg add	git add[d]	vv add
Edit			git add[e]	
Delete	svn delete	hg remove	git rm	vv remove
Rename	svn move	hg rename	git mv	vv rename
Move	svn move	hg rename	git mv	vv move
Status	svn status	hg status	git status	vv status
Diff	svn diff	hg diff	git diff	vv diff
Revert	svn revert	hg revert	[f]	vv revert
Log	svn log	hg log	git log	vv log
Tag	svn copy[g]	hg tag[h]	git tag	vv tag[i]
Branch	svn copy[j]	hg branch	git branch	vv branch
Merge	svn merge	hg merge	git merge	vv merge
Resolve	svn resolve	hg resolve		vv resolve
Lock	svn lock	[k]	[l]	vv lock[m]
Clone		hg clone	git clone	vv clone
Push		hg push[n]	git push[o]	vv push[p]
Pull		hg pull[q]	git fetch[r]	vv pull[s]

[a] In Mercurial, the repository instance is stored inside working copy.

[b] In Git, the repository instance is stored inside working copy.

[c] Without -a, commits only those things which have been explicitly added to the git index.

[d] **git add** is also used to notify Git of a modified file.

[e]Or, automatic when using **git commit -a**.

[f]**git checkout** can be used to revert the contents of a file. There is a **git revert** command but it is used to alter changesets that have already been committed.

[g]Tag appears as a directory in the repository tree. Causes a commit.

[h]Tags are stored in a version-controlled text file. Causes a commit.

[i]Tags are stored in a database DAG.

[j]Branch appears as a directory in the repository tree. Causes a commit.

[k]Lock is unsupported by Mercurial.

[l]Lock is unsupported by Git.

[m]Requires network connection to the upstream repository instance.

[n]Requires --new-branch when pushing a new branch.

[o]By default, pushes only the branches which already exist on the other side.

[p]By default, pushes all changesets in all DAGs.

[q]Does not update the working copy without -u.

[r]**git pull** is equivalent to **pull** followed by **update**.

[s]Does not update the working copy without -u.

Glossary

acyclic
> Not cyclic.
> See Also cyclic.

add
> Add a file or directory to the pending changeset; tell the VCS to begin tracking changes to a file or directory.

administrative area
> Typically, a hidden directory within a working copy where the VCS stores state information.

atomic commit
> A commit operation which entirely succeeds or entirely fails. In other words, no matter how many individual modifications are in the pending changeset, after the commit operation, the repository will either end up with all of them (if the operation is successful), or none of them (if the operation fails).

audit
> In Veracity, a record which stores when a changeset was created and the userid of the user who created it.

blimey
> Term to express surprise or excitement; corruption of "Blind me".

blob
> Binary Large Object; a sequence of bytes.

Bob's your uncle
> A commonly used British expression which indicates success at the end of a list of instructions.

box
> See idiot's lantern.

BR-549
> Short and easy-to-remember phone number of Samples Sales, Junior Samples' fictional used car dealership on *Hee Haw*, an American variety television series.

branch
> Create another line of development.

Brummagem
> The local dialect of Birmingham, England; bears a passing resemblance to English.

Brummies
> Residents or natives of Birmingham, England. Notable specimens include Neville Chamberlain, Ozzy Osbourne, Steve Winwood, Digby Jones, and Nathan Delfouneso.

burn down chart
> In iteration based development, a diagram which shows the work completed and the predicted track for the tasks in the current iteration of the project.

C99
> A dialect of the C programming language, standardized by ISO and ANSI around 1999, over ten years ago, and yet, the Microsoft C compiler **still** doesn't support it.

Cairo filesystem
> An object filesystem which was never released, despite it being shown to attendees of the 1993 Microsoft Professional Developers Conference.

canonical stuff
> Any piece of data which is not automatically derived from another piece of data.

centralized
> Describes a version control system which requires an active connection with a single central server for most operations.

changelog
> In Mercurial, the revlog which contains all the changesets for a repository.

changeset
> A set of changes which should be treated as an indivisible group; the list of differences between one version of the repository tree and the next version.

checkin
> A synonym for commit, used by some version control tools.

checkout
> Create a working copy.

chuffed
> Pleased or delighted.

clone
> Create a new repository instance that is a copy of another.

closet
> In Veracity, the name of the area where repository instances are stored.

collision
> With respect to cryptographic hashes, when two different input values result in the same hash result.

comma
> Punctuation mark used primarily for separation of list entries and clauses; practically impossible to use consistently and the cause of many altercations between commaphiles and commaphobes.

commit
> Apply the modifications in the working copy to the repository as a new changeset.

commit
> To make a new revision of the repository by incorporating a new changeset.

continuous integration
> The process of automatically building and testing a software project after every commit.

Crabapple Cove, Maine
> The fictional home town of Hawkeye Pierce in *M*A*S*H*.

create

Create a new, empty repository.

cryptographic hash

A short digest (typically 160, 256, or 512 bits in length) which is computed from an arbitrarily large piece of data using an algorithm that makes it infeasible to create two different pieces of data with the same digest.

CVCS

Centralized Version Control System; a general term used when referring to the class of version control systems which require a single central server.

CVS

Concurrent Versions System; a second generation version control tool which was extremely popular. With Subversion having largely succeeded in its goal of being "a compelling replacement for CVS", most people in the industry would agree that CVS usage is in decline.

cyclic

See looping.

DAG

directed acyclic graph.

dagnum

In Veracity, a hexadecimal identifier for a DAG.

data

Plural form of datum; commonly used by authors as a singular noun, often over the objections of their editors.

decentralized

Describes a version control system which allows each node to operate independently, without the need for active communication with a single central server.

deduplication

The removal of duplicate copies of data through the use of cryptographic hashes.

deflate

The compression algorithm used by zlib. Veracity uses deflate for blob storage.

delete

Delete a file or directory in the working copy, adding the deletion to the pending changeset.

delta

An expression of the difference between two pieces of data.

diff

Show the details of the modifications that have been made to the working copy.

DiffMerge

A free (gratis) application for comparing and merging text files, created and distributed by SourceGear, supported on Mac, Windows, and Linux.

digest

See cryptographic hash.

directed acyclic graph

A data structure with a series of nodes, each of which may have directed edges (arrows) pointing to other nodes, so long as the arrows never form a cycle.

DocBook

The XML-based markup language I am using as I write this book. I do all of my editing of the XML file with vim. The DocBook XML is then processed with xsltproc and the docbook-xsl-1.76.1 stylesheets, which can generate a variety of formats. For the printed edition, the stylesheets generate an FO file which is converted to a press-ready PDF/X-1a file by Antenna House Formatter v5.3.

Don't Panic!

The best advice given to humanity by Douglas Adams; also one of the catch phrases of Lance-Corporal Jones on the British comedy television series *Dad's Army*.

doss

Same as faff, if you're a Brummie.

DVCS

Decentralized (or Distributed) Version Control System; a general term used when referring to the class of version control systems which are decentralized.

edit
> Modify a file in the working copy. Some version control tools need to be explicitly notified that the user wants to modify a file or that a file has already been modified. Others detect modified files automatically.

eight-day clock
> I have no idea what this means, but apparently Southern folks say it, and it sounds funny.

England
> Current country and former nation-state formed from the unification of the Kingdoms of East Anglia, Essex, Kent, Mercia, Northumbira, Sussex, and Wessex. Home to numerous dialects and slang terms, and the country with the most sane rules for using punctuation with quotations.

faff
> To waste time.

feature branch
> A branch which is used specifically for the development of one feature.

FS3
> In Veracity, the name of an implementation of the repository storage API.

Futilisoft
> A fictional software company I made up for the examples in this book.

GID
> In Veracity, Global ID. The concatenation of the letter 'g' plus a type 4 UUID plus a type 1 UUID.

gunter
> To repair.

head
> The tip of a branch; a node on a named branch which has no children that are also members of the same named branch.

hg
> The name of the Mercurial command-line app.

HID

In Veracity, Hash ID. A hexadecimal (all lower case) expression of a crypto-graphic hash.

hospital

"It's a big building with patients, but that's not important right now."

Howzat?

Common appeal to a cricket umpire by a bowler or fielder; corruption of "How's that?".

idiot's lantern

See telly.

indent

A utility that reformats C code.

JSON

JavaScript Object Notation; a JavaScript-based syntax for representing objects with named properties and arrays.

Keep calm and carry on

Slogan on a British morale-boosting poster produced at the start of the Second World War.

kerfuffle

Disturbance or disruption.

label

A synonym for tag, used by some version control tools.

landlady face

Facial expression like that of a landlady trying to collect overdue rent; indicative of displeasure or ill-humour.

last wicket

The dismissal of the tenth batsman, resulting in the end of a cricket innings.

leaf node

A DAG node which has no children.

lock
> Prevent other people from modifying a file.

lock
> A mechanism used to prevent other users from modifying a file.

log
> Show the history of changes to the repository.

looping
> See cyclic.

manifest
> In Mercurial, the list of all files in a revision of the repository.

master branch
> The main line of development. In Mercurial this is called "default".

merge
> Apply changes from one branch to another.
> Combine two versions of a file or directory into one by appropriately incorporating the changes made in both versions.

mithering
> Irritation or bother.

move
> Move a file or directory in the working copy, adding the move operation to the pending changeset.

named branch
> A named line of development within a version control DAG. Named branches allow multiple lines of development to exist within a single repository instance. An alternate style of branching with a DVCS is to keep one branch per repository instance, though this approach is considered less flexible.

nark
> State of annoyance or irritation.

obliterate
> To alter the history of a version control repository by completely removing something that was previously committed.

Ottumwa, Iowa
    The non-fictional home town of Radar O'Reilly in *M*A*S*H*.

parents
    If a DAG node D is derived from DAG nodes B and C, then B and C are said to be the parents of D.

pending changeset
    The changes which have been made to a working copy but which have not yet been committed to a repository instance.

plump turkey in November
    Likely doomed to end in somebody's belly for the Thanksgiving holiday in the United States.

polishing branch
    A temporary branch which is used during the time that a team is polishing software to get it ready for a release.

Pond, the
    Large body of water east of Halifax, Nova Scotia; better known as the Atlantic Ocean.

Powerball
    A lottery in the United States.

pull
    Copy changesets from a remote repository instance to a local one. Does not affect working copies.

push
    Copy changesets from a local repository instance to a remote one. Does not affect working copies.

put paid to
    To complete or finish a task.

Pyrenean Gold Press
    The small publishing identity I created because I am too much of a control freak to work with an existing publisher.

RCS
: Revision Control System; the second version control system, first released in 1982.

release branch
: A branch which contains the code/content which exactly corresponds to a released version of software.

rename
: Rename a file or directory in the working copy, adding the rename operation to the pending changeset.

repository
: An archive which contains every version of the tree which has ever been committed, plus metadata about who did the commit, when it was done, and why.

repository instance
: In a DVCS, a specific copy of the repository.

resolve
: Handle conflicts resulting from a merge.

revert
: Undo modifications that have been made to the working copy.

revlog
: In Mercurial, the file format which stores all revisions of a file.

root dagnode
: The first node of a DAG; the node which has no parents.

Samples, Junior
: Honest as the day is long; unable to pronounce "trigonometry".

SCCS
: Source Code Control System; the first version control system, created in 1972.

Scrum
: An iteration-based methodology for software development.

SHA-1
> A 160 bit cryptographic hash function which was a government standard in the United States until it was replaced by SHA-2. Considered obsolete for many applications.

SHA-2
> A family of cryptographic hash functions. SHA-2 is a government standard in the United States. SHA-2 can be used to create digests of 224, 256, 384, or 512 bits.

shambolic
> Chaotic; disorganized.

ship-shape and Bristol fashion
> Immaculately in order; all components of a larger whole in their proper place.

shrinkwrap
> Software that is licensed to be installed on computers owned by the customer.

Skein
> A family of cryptographic hash functions created by Bruce Schneier and others. At the time of this writing, Skein is a candidate in the competition to select a hash algorithm which will become SHA-3.

skiving off
> Pretending to be working while doing nothing useful.

SourceGear
> The software company where I work.

Spit the bit
> To grow tired and give less effort.

status
> List the modifications that have been made to the working copy.

sticky wicket
> Literally a damp playing surface for the game of cricket; slang term for any difficult situation.

svn
> The name of the Subversion command-line app.

tag
> Associate a meaningful name with a specific version in the repository.

telly
> Television.

template
> In Veracity, a JSON object which specifies the record types for a decentralized database.

treenode
> In Veracity, a JSON object which lists the contents of a directory under version control.

uniqify
> In Veracity, to automatically resolve the violation of a unique constraint, using instructions from a template.

update
> Update the working copy with respect to the repository.

UUID
> Universally Unique Identifier.

vcdiff
> A binary delta algorithm described in RFC 3284[1].

VCS
> Version Control System; a generic term used when referring to any version control system.

Veracity
> An open source distributed version control system created by SourceGear.

vscript
> In Veracity, the name of the command-line application for executing scripts.

vv
> The name of the Veracity command-line app.

---

[1]http://tools.ietf.org/html/rfc3284

whinge
> To complain persistently.

wicket
> A cricket term with several distinct meanings: the sets of wooden stumps protected by batsmen; the act of dismissing a batsman (similar to a baseball "out" for Americans); or the playing surface itself.

working copy
> A snapshot of a specific revision of the repository tree, owned by a single user, for the purpose of making modifications which may be committed to the repository to create a new revision.

Wumpty
> West Midlands Passenger Transport Executive (WMPTE); the Birmingham-area bus authority, also slang for "bus" itself.

Zawinski's Law
> "Every program attempts to expand until it can read mail. Those programs which cannot so expand are replaced by ones which can."

Index